TRANSITION HOUSE, 1976-2017.

TRANSITION HOUSE, 1976-2017.

The Movement and The Mainstream

ANN FLECK-HENDERSON

TABLE OF CONTENTS

Introduction

What we know as Transition House began in conversations in Cambridge in 1975, in the midst of a feminist movement that birthed many organizations and fundamentally changed our culture. Forty years later, it is a very different organization from the organization of its founders. In its early years, it was a movement organization, largely secret, firmly resisting a social service identity; a collective, opposing a hierarchical governance structure; a peer-help organization, rejecting a mental health perspective on violence; a women-only space. Today it is a community-involved social service organization with a traditional governance structure including social workers among its staff and interns. There are men on staff, and occasionally men are residents in the shelter. Since 1976 Transition House has struggled to stay loyal to its original principles while adapting to the realities of a context that was changing, partly because of the success of its earlier efforts.

A long-ago cartoonish drawing has the caption: "Inside every older person is a younger person ... wondering what happened."[1] As Transition House continues into its fourth decade, some of its earlier participants might wonder, "What happened?" This book is partly documentation of Transition House's history as I have come to know it, and partly an attempt at insight into answering the question of "What happened?"

Background of the Book

As a Cambridge resident and a survivor of domestic violence in the years before it had a name, I was aware of Transition House since it opened its doors in January 1976. Only after I retired (as a professor of social work) did I get to know Transition House in any depth. Inspired by its current work,

---

1   Brilliant, A. (1991). *I Have Abandoned My Search for the Truth, and Am Now Looking for a Good Fantasy.* Woodbridge Press: Santa Barbara, CA. p. 62.

conscious of its proud past, and aware that many of the important players in its evolution were still alive, I asked if anyone had written its history. No one had; an anniversary was approaching; I volunteered.

I began by looking at the Transition House materials at the Arthur and Elizabeth Schlesinger Library on the History of Women in America in Cambridge, Mass. The library's holdings include documents from the early years of Transition House and videotapes made in or near 1976.

In the Spring of 2013, Risa Mednick, Transition House's current executive director (ED) organized a project "launch," to which we invited anyone we could find who had played a significant role, past or present, in Transition House. The event served as a reunion for many people who had not seen each other for years. The assembled guests added to a time line posted on the walls of the room in which we met, and each person spoke briefly about her or his experience at Transition House. Some of those present had filled multiple roles over many years; many expressed their gratitude to others, some present, some absent, for the transformative effect Transition House had had on their lives. At that event a number of people mentioned that they had papers from their years in the collective and/or on the board, which they were willing to give or loan to me for this project.

Since that day I have collected and read file boxes full of papers and interviewed more than 60 people who played important, and less important, roles in the life of Transition House, or "T House," as it is often called. A few of those I interviewed were or had been clients/residents of Transition House. Those most important voices are not easy to locate, as confidentiality has kept their names from any records, and I am particularly grateful to the former and current clients who were willing to speak with me about their experiences. I am grateful as well to the many women (and a few men) who had worked at or with Transition House and gave of their time for an interview, usually between one and two hours in duration. These included most of the staff at the time of the interviews (2013-14 and 2017).

I have tried to present Transition House's history in a way that is both readable and includes most of the information to which I had access. In some ways, these are not mutually compatible objectives. Except in this introduction and in the conclusion, I have minimized my own voice. Where there were differing perspectives and opinions among those I interviewed, I have tried to include the diversity of views.

There are many quotes from the people who spoke with me. In most cases, the speaker is identified by her role at Transition House and not by name, and most of the quotes reflect sentiments or information I heard from more than one person. To keep the number of footnotes manageable, I have made a specific attribution with a footnote only when the quote includes something controversial or is from written or videotaped material. There is a list at the end of those I interviewed. There are also key people with whom I did not speak, either because I did not know of them or could not find them, or I simply ran out of time. I hope these people will find the document true also to their experiences.

The narrative is organized chronologically. The first two sections are on the 1970s and 1980s, each with its conclusion section. The 1990s section ends in 1998, with the end of the collective. The end of the collective marked a major turning point, and it seemed necessary to start a new section with the "pivotal years" of 1998-1999. The narrative for the years since 1998 is broken into sections that reflect major shifts for Transition House. You will not find parallel headings under each time period, logical though that might have been. Each period had such different challenges and accomplishments that I could not make a parallel structure fit. I thought I was finished in November 2015, with a document in time for the 40th anniversary of Transition House. It may be fortunate that various delays gave me time and opportunity to research and write the final chapter, without which this would be, in 2017, a very incomplete record. The years between 2015 and 2017 have again seen major changes.

This is *a* history of Transition House. I have tried to represent faithfully the thoughts and reflections of the many people I interviewed as well as the material I have from files of volunteers, staff, and/or board members. Particularly with respect to the written material, there are gaps, years with little in writing, and gluts. Not surprisingly, generally, there is less written material from the collective years, and much more from recent years. Although I tried to compensate for the gaps and gluts, they undoubtedly affect my sense of the history. Interviewees were given the opportunity to review a draft of this history, make corrections and/or point out omissions, and a number of them did. In every case I accepted those suggestions and believe this increases the book's credibility.

CHAPTER 1

1970s: We Will Not Be Beaten

Beginnings, 1975-1976

In January 1976, two women, both mothers of young children and on welfare, opened their apartment as a refuge for other women fleeing domestic violence. That event marks the start of Transition House. Of course, it was not really the beginning. The context of what is known as the second wave feminist movement—in Cambridge, Mass., nationally and internationally[2]—and the particular journeys of a few women made that event possible.

Betsy Warrior, a single mother with a 10th grade formal education, had fled a violent marriage and was living in Cambridge in 1968. She saw a newspaper advertisement calling on women to start a female liberation front that would "abolish all male supremacist institutions."[3] That ad led her to become one of the founding members of Cell 16, a group of dedicated radical feminists. In that group of women, Betsy read a lot and wrote a lot. She remarked, "I started working on a theory of housework and how women are economically enslaved ... and I decided that this was a key to women's oppression worldwide...but as I was doing this work, I became more and more aware ... that women were beaten, constantly and consistently, housewives were beaten. I was beaten myself for years. That's what finally forced me out of the marriage."[4, 5] In 1969, she published *Housework: Slavery or a Labor of Love* in which she noted that wife-beating was an occupational hazard of being an unpaid laborer (housewife) without independent resources to escape.

---

2   See Schechter, S. (1982). *Women and Male Violence,* Boston: South End Press, chapter 2 for an excellent summary.

3   Typed Founders' Meeting Transcript (FMT), undated, probably around 1990, p. 1.

4   Ibid, p. 2.

5   Ibid, p. 3.

During these same years, local women were expressing their increasing frustrations and gaining power through other local initiatives. In 1971 women took over a Harvard University building, protesting the lack of resources for women at Harvard and Massachusetts Institute of Technology (MIT) and aligning with neighborhood residents in demanding (among other things) low-cost housing. That takeover, captured in a recent documentary, *Left on Pearl,* led to the founding of the Cambridge Women's Center on Pleasant Street. A group of women who formally incorporated as the Boston Women's Health Book Collective in 1972 produced the first editions of the groundbreaking book *Our Bodies, Ourselves: A Book by and for Women* in the early 1970s. After meetings at the Women's Center, the Boston Area Rape Crisis Center started there in 1973. In 1974, in nearby Somerville, women provided support to other women fleeing violence by creating support groups and safe homes under the name "RESPOND." The terms "battered women" and "domestic violence" were just coming into the US vocabulary.

Betsy Warrior's article *Battered Lives* appeared in 1974 among the first published materials on battering. A friend took copies to the first National Organization for Women conference, where they were "snatched up."[6] Also in that year, Women's Advocates, often deemed the first dedicated domestic violence shelter in the United States,[7] opened in St. Paul, Minn.[8]

By 1974 Betsy had a young collaborator in Lisa Leghorn. Lisa had attended Cell 16 meetings in the late 1960s while finishing high school in Boston, then left the area for some years, returning in 1973. With her publications circulating, Betsy began hearing from women all over the country with information about what other groups were doing and received requests to speak. Lisa did much of the speaking. Betsy continued to write, compiling information related to battering. The first of a series of the *Battered Women's Directory,* formerly called *Working on Wife Abuse,* appeared in April 1976. While they were working together, Betsy and Lisa heard about two women in Cambridge who were planning to open their apartment to women fleeing abuse.

---

6   Ibid, p. 5.

7   Haven House, a shelter started by women in Al-Anon for abused wives of alcoholics, opened in California in 1964, quite separate from the women's movement. See Schechter, 1982, *Women and Male Violence,* Boston: South End Press, p. 55. Some time lines suggest there may have been one or two other early shelters that did not manage to make it into historical accounts.

8   Women's Advocates. (1980). *Women's Advocates: The Story of a Shelter.* Self-published: MN. p. 1.

Chris Womendez and Cherie Jimenez had both fled violent husbands. Cherie had left Puerto Rico, her husband's home, for Canada, hoping to stay there with her young child. Finding that impossible, she returned to her native United States. On the return trip she stopped in Toronto at a refuge for women, which made a big impression. In Cambridge, and on welfare, she happened to rent an apartment downstairs from Chris Womendez, another young mother on welfare who had fled abuse. They talked together about creating a refuge in Cambridge and began meeting with a group of friends to plan for it. Chris was taking a law class, and a class teaching assistant agreed to meet with the group. For about a year a small group (sometimes only three women) had weekly meetings in Chris' living room. Betsy Warrior and Lisa Leghorn started to meet with them.

"There were so many things going on," Cherie said, thinking back. "The Women's Center was around the corner; the food co-op; the farm workers' movement. It was an exciting time. Somehow we came to the conclusion to open the downstairs apartment [as a shelter]." Toward the end of 1975 Chris and Cherie decided to "just do it."

From the Founders Meeting Transcript:

> Chris: Well, I was living on the second floor with this friend of mine, and she and I shared a Section 8 apartment together. So, we split that rent which was nothing. It was like fifty dollars or something like that. We were both on AFDC [Aid to Families with Dependent Children, a former federal assistance program]. We both had children. We were both lesbian mothers. And ... Cherie was living downstairs paying full rent.

> Cherie: I had the apartment downstairs, and it wasn't a big apartment, but it was five rooms, and that's when we decided that we could use that apartment.... [W]e made bunk beds, and we decided that we would just open up the apartment and not go through this bureaucratic way of dealing with things and just do it.

> Chris: We planned it before we opened the apartment, we met with lawyers once a week, working out all the fine points: what happens if somebody's husband comes into your apartment and they kill the woman they're looking for, all the different little nitty-gritties, we worked on it, all the fine points. We also met with all kinds of people, six months prior to opening up our apartment ... all kinds of people

in the community, we had meetings in our living room all the time. We sent letters out, bulk mailed letters, like massive letter writings to all of the broken bone units in hospitals …We put posters up inside of the laundromats, inside of the bathrooms of the broken bones units, inside of maternity ward waiting rooms, inside of anything we could think of where there may be a battered woman, all of the legal aid places received letters from us. So, we spent six months working our butt off, and Betsy helped a lot with that."

Friends who had been part of the earlier discussions in the apartment also publicized the opening of the refuge on TV and radio. Chris and Cherie opened the doors on January 1, 1976. The calls came, and then the women and children. Lots of women and children. Chris and Cherie recall the details and set the tone of what it was like to be in the house in those initial days:

Chris: So January 1ˢᵗ, 1976 we opened the door. We spent New Year's Eve still working on it, right up until the last minute. And then that morning, we received our first woman. We had our locks all built, everything was all set up. We had stacks of mattresses that were in the closet in the daytime, but covered the kitchen and living room floors in the evening. And we were ready. So our first woman came in who was battered by her son, believe it or not, not her husband. We just went on from there. Before we knew it, the place was packed with people: babies were crying, and people were on the phone. There were just people, people everywhere.

Cherie: Women were also very excited … this is the first time anybody heard of a place that women could go to. So, just the fact that they were kind of excited about seeing something like this. And the fact that they were there in the beginning. In spite of the chaoticness [sic] … in the difficult time, people also tried to help when they stayed there, they would also try to help with things, with the kids, and they understood the situation.

Chris: But this was sort of different in a way [than] if a woman walks into a shelter now…. It was almost like they walked into the heart of the women's movement itself, because Transition House became like the heart of the women's movement. …everything was so intertwined.[9]

---

9   Typed Founders' Meeting Transcript (FMT), undated, probably around 1990.

Chris and Cherie attempted to staff the apartment 24 hours a day, seven days a week. They or their friends picked up women and children from neutral locations, once they realized the risks in going to the women's homes. Food stamps and AFDC benefits were pooled to buy food and supplies. Lisa Leghorn wrote:

> At times ... there were as many as 25 women and children staying with them, sleeping on mattresses on living room and kitchen floors as well as in the three bedrooms. The women were of all nationalities, races and class backgrounds. Some stayed a few days until they could find friends or relatives to go to, others a month or more; one woman stayed four months and is now committed to continuing work with the house, as are many of the other women.[10]

When a new woman came to the house, she was taken to the one room that was kept quiet to hear a tape recording made by one of the first residents about her experience. The woman who made the tape was the wife of a police officer and mother of five. In a calm voice, and with some humor, she recorded what it was like to live in the apartment, her experience when she came, what she was doing now. She explained about local playgrounds, schools. It helped the new women to relax and know what to expect. It also instilled hope that they would get through the transitional time and painful experience. When a woman could not manage in the communal setting, possibly because of mental illness, friends who had apartments nearby could sometimes take her in. In their interviews Chris and Cherie explained the energy felt at Transition House: "Women were idealistic, seeing a whole new kind of life. [It was] chaotic, crazy, good," Chris recalled. Cherie agreed, "It was power back, energy from being part of a movement. We are part of it! It's happening! We had the sense that it was greater than a program or a shelter. It was women together, solidarity."

In a videotaped interview (possibly 1976), Cherie described both the chaos and the power of those months: "It makes women feel strong if they don't have to rely on men or corporations or big money. No one got paid. It was really informal. Everyone who stayed helped. They realized they weren't alone. You can do things that everyone said you can't do. It was all run by women coming in and women in the neighborhood and friends."[11]

The constant responsibility and shared living space was hard on Chris

---

10   Leghorn, L., (1976). "Transition House Shelters Battered Women." *Sojourner*, October 1976, p. 8.

11   VT13: Videotape, ca. 1976, Schlesinger Library.

and Cherie and on their own children, with whom they also had less time. Occasionally, they would seek more privacy at friends' apartments. After six months, both Chris and Cherie were exhausted. Realizing they had to reorganize to distribute the work differently, they stopped taking in new women. Although the landlord had been aware of what they were doing, neighbors began to complain. In June, they were forced to close the shelter, although a few women stayed on in the apartment. By then, however, the movement to shelter battered women had gained force.

Working with Betsy and Lisa and their feminist colleagues, the Women's Center, in August 1976, announced plans for a Women Supporting Women demonstration to mark the anniversary of the passage of women's suffrage on August 26, 1920. The demonstration was to focus specifically on violence against women, particularly married women.[12] That demonstration, which occurred shortly after Chris and Cherie had to close their apartment, was critical to the next phase of Transition House's life. (Figure 1: August March.)

About 5,000 people demonstrated, and women who had stayed at the apartment spoke in front of them. The crowd was responsive and supportive. The excitement for the organizers was intense. As Betsy explained: "We felt like we were on the cusp of a revolution, that everything and anything was possible. I remember, at that time and before, we were thinking for quite a while that if we just pushed far enough, if we just reached enough people and made enough people conscious, that there would be a complete overthrow of male supremacy, and that's really how we were feeling sort of then."[13] During the summer of 1976, when Boston women held their demonstration, Women's Advocates had been open in St. Paul for more than a year. The planning group in Cambridge communicated with the women in St. Paul, as did other groups around the country.

The apartment experience had demonstrated the need for a shelter and politicized many formerly battered women. Pledge letters promised $300 a month. About 20 people volunteered on the spot to work at the shelter. Donations started coming in—mostly small ones, but a great many. Fund-raising continued, and by September they had raised enough money to rent a house. The core planning group, larger by now, worked into the fall.

Chris and Cherie had decided not to live at the new house, which led to questions of how to staff the shelter. The work of running it was to be done primarily by volunteers in committees. The original committees were:

---

12 *On Our Way*, Cambridge Women's Center newsletter, Summer 1976.

13 Betsy Warrior in FMT, p. 52.

Figure 1: August March.

fund-raising, community outreach and education, volunteer screening and training, maintenance, child care, and house search. Based on the apartment experience, the group knew that problems and issues tend to arise at night and decided there should be 24-hour coverage in shifts. Because there would be no person who was consistently present, new structures would be needed for communication. The group decided to implement and maintain a house log and a phone log for volunteers. Volunteers were responsible for recording all important events of the day in the house log. At the start of a new shift, volunteers were expected to read all entries written since they were last on-site. The planning group had hoped to rely solely on formerly battered women as volunteers, but it seemed more important to get started than to limit the volunteer pool to those who had themselves experienced violence. So, they broadened the criteria to any interested woman who was willing to make the commitment.

Volunteers needed to be trained before the house opened. Trainings included information on philosophy and history, duties while on shift, legal and welfare advocacy. Role-playing of crisis calls and advocacy were added later. "Philosophy and history" included an analysis of systemic oppression that focused on patriarchy, but also spoke about race and class oppression. "Our purpose," said one early volunteer, "was both to minister to women and to be the revolution."

For many volunteers, as for many other Americans, a social analysis of oppression was completely new and eye-opening. Volunteers from more privileged backgrounds often examined their own assumptions about race and class for the first time. Speaking about her experience of the training, one long-time volunteer reported discovering "assumptions I never knew I had." For those from more oppressed backgrounds, the training was an affirmation of what they knew but had not articulated.

The planning group was constrained by time, which led to the decision to rent, not buy, a house.[14] Although the house would be staffed and run primarily by volunteers, the group applied for and received a $1200 grant to pay one full-time staff person for four months to get the shelter up and running. Transition House opened its doors as a project of the Women's Center in a rented house on Elm Street in November 1976. It was one of the first dedicated domestic violence shelters in the United States, and the first in New England.

The Shelter and The Collective

By the time the shelter opened, about 30 people staffed it and volunteered there. Although Chris and Cherie reduced their role to weekly meetings with the residents, many people who had been involved since the earlier days of the project contributed to its continuity. The staff (a few paid; most volunteers) had their own weekly meeting.

The first "welcome sheet" explained that the length of stay was four weeks for women without children and six weeks for women with children; "hopefully this is enough time to allow you to find a new apartment, get financial

---

14   VT13: Videotape, ca. 1976, Schlesinger Library.

assistance, or find a job."[15] (In 1976 these were realistic expectations.) Women with income were expected to contribute for food. House meetings were held once a week. The sheet clarified procedures and expectations: "Someone will be meeting with you informally to see how we can help you with services, and mothers should explain the rules of the house to their children. ...There are few rules here, but women are generally asked to help each other, to keep the house clean...."[16] The philosophy of the house was one of self-help and peer help. Women staying at the shelter were referred to as guests. The values of the house were made clear: "Women do a lot of advocacy for each other, e.g. go with each other to court. This is one of the most important things."[17]

Most of the women seeking shelter arrived after talking with a volunteer/ staff person on the hotline. (Both volunteers and paid staff were referred to as "staff.") If the caller was ready to leave her home and come to shelter, the staff person strategized with her about when and how to leave her home safely. If there was a room for her at the shelter, the staff person on the hotline arranged for the caller to be picked up in a central location by another staff person. As other shelters in Massachusetts developed, the policy was to refer a caller to a shelter outside her own community. Thus, Cambridge residents calling Transition House were referred elsewhere.

Lynne was then a young mother of two small children, living with her boyfriend in the Boston area in 1976. She detailed the experiences that led her to Transition House:

> I was from the Midwest. He brought me to Massachusetts as he had friends there. I had no family or friends and no social life in Massachusetts. I was insecure and had low self-esteem.

> The relationship was not abusive in the beginning, but the relationship was not a positive one and was not heading into a positive direction such as marriage. Then he became very jealous and accusatory. He accused me of seeing other men. He made statements like "didn't I see you riding in a blue car?" and "why do you have to go to the store now, are you going to meet someone?" All of this made me second guess myself.

> Nothing can really prepare you on how to react to being beaten by

---

15 FMT, p. 42.

16 Ibid, p. 43.

17 VT6: Videotape, ca. 1976. Schlesinger Library.

someone who you trusted. He would choke me and gave me numerous black eyes and threatened to put me in the hospital. And there was no rhyme or reason on what would make him angry.

One day after a very scary night of his abuse, I called a hotline and told the person what I was going through and they gave me an address of a refuge in the Cambridge area. I grabbed my children and my pocketbook and left the apartment. I stayed at this refuge for about 4 days. There I met other women who had gotten out of abusive relationships. Staying at this refuge gave me a ray of hope that things could get better for me. However, I realized that I needed to go back to my apartment to get important papers and clothes for us. So I went back to my apartment, and I was able to communicate with my batterer; but I am sure we both knew that the relationship was over. After a few weeks of being with him, I got the courage to get out for good. He had left the apartment to go somewhere, and as soon as he left, I called the hotline again and was instructed to go to a location in the Cambridge area and that someone would take me to Transition House. After talking to the hotline, I called the police and told them my situation and that I needed an officer to escort me out of the apartment. I wanted to leave the apartment, but I did not want him returning as I was trying to leave. It wasn't like he would just let me pack my bags and say goodbye. I then called a taxi to take me to Cambridge. The police officer was very kind and watched me as I loaded up my children, three large bags of clothes and a couple bags of food into the taxi. The taxi driver dropped us off in Cambridge and the rest is history or herstory.

I became immersed in the women's movement and helping other battered women. Transition House saw some qualities in me and offered me a job working with the women and answering the crisis line. Betsy Warrior and I facilitated a support group for battered women.[18]

Women staying at Transition House used the Women's Center address to receive mail and the Women's Center resources for finding housing, jobs, and other needed services. Because the official address was that of the Women's Center, men looking to find their sheltered partners more frequently appeared

---

18   From an interview with Lynne, June 2015, edited by her for inclusion here.

there than at Elm Street. The collective hoped to buy a property, but there was some concern that the stakes around secrecy would be even higher. A Women's Center activist who worked with the Transition House group reflected on the risk of owning a house: "If someone finds it, what do you do? Sell the house?"

Staff members established a schedule made at the beginning of each week to cover the day-to-day staffing of that week. Volunteers were asked for a commitment of at least six to 12 months that included attendance at meetings every week. In special cases, volunteers could meet every other week. Volunteers worked in five-hour shifts on the hotline and/or with the guests in the shelter. The office was in the building, and guests could stop by and chat with the volunteer responsible for managing the hotline at a given time.

The staff initially envisioned that all decisions would be made collectively by all participants— guests, volunteers, and paid staff. It soon became clear that most of the guests were too busy dealing with the crises in their own lives to give time to collective meetings, which tended to be lengthy. As early as 1977, there was an attempt to restructure; the staff created 1) a "core collective" representing all committees and those most involved in the functioning of the house, 2) a larger staff meeting for all volunteers who could attend, and 3) a meeting of the whole including guests.

All the women in the most committed core group worked far more hours than what is considered a "normal" work week. They were organizing and staffing a shelter and building a movement. The work included: community education and fund-raising; working shifts at the shelter and on the hotline, organizing volunteers, picking up new guests, accompanying guests to court and other commitments, repairing plumbing, getting food, and dealing with crises in the house. In addition, some of the staff travelled to conferences, participated in radio and TV interviews, and worked on national newsletters and projects. One of the early group recalled, "Externally, it was such a struggle; and internally, it was such a struggle; but such a wonderful family. The work ethic was tyrannical."

Within the first year at Elm Street, a radio campaign on radio station WEEI brought in enough money for a down payment on a house that was to be, and remains today, a permanent residence for the shelter. The property cost $24,000. The low price reflected the terrible condition of the house, which was, as one volunteer said, "in tough shape." In keeping with their conviction about the value of self-help and their practice of making the most out of every dollar, the women of the collective did most of the renovations themselves. (Figure 2: Front of House).

Figure 2: Front of House

It is likely that, in late 1970s, a crew of women rehabilitating a house on a city street in Cambridge attracted some attention, but somehow the nature of the project was kept secret, and the work stayed "under the radar" of city officials and police and fire departments. One friend in City Hall "greased the wheels" so the rehabbing could go forward without too many questions being asked. The Transition House staff mistrusted official (i.e., male) authority, a mistrust reinforced by early experience with battered wives of police officers.

For a brief period during the transition from the house on Elm Street to the new house, the hotline operated out of a volunteer's apartment, staffed by two volunteers, while the shelter was without a home. All other staff and volunteers and some guests were working on rehabilitating the new building.

Women staying in the house, with support from the staff, did the work of the house, such as cooking, cleaning, and caring for the children. One room upstairs was the office where a volunteer also answered the hotline. Guests drifted in and out of the office space for informal chats with the people working there. Staff and volunteers moved comfortably around the house, joining groups of women in the kitchen or the children in the play area. It was "a continuing support group," which included "constant informal group work." The official house meeting for residents took place after breakfast each day, at which the women made plans for the day for themselves and for the house.

The staff made an effort to give each family its own room. Sometimes an emergency call would come in, and there were no available beds. If there was nowhere else to send the caller, the staff gathered the guests in the house to get consensus to allow the caller to stay on the couch. Usually, the answer was yes; it was difficult to say no.

Guests gave Transition House its shortened name: One of the early volunteers recalled, "The name 'T House' was a code word that a group of residents started using so as not to give away our location."[19]

The battered women's movement had focused on women, without paying much attention to children, and most volunteers came to help the women without thinking about the children. Rachel Burger, an artist who had joined the original group and stayed through the 1980s, focused on the children in the shelter and the need for a children's program. Rachel initiated the children's program—among the first structured children's programs in a shelter—in 1978. Staff members were also trained to respond gently, but clearly, to women who were harsh or violent to their children. The staff hired a coordinator for a parenting skills program in 1979, and women could continue to receive parenting support after leaving the program. Transition House also collaborated with the Black Ecumenical Council, a foster grandparent program, beginning that year.[20]

Philosophically, the group was opposed to making rules for the women staying in the house. Women seeking shelter were escaping situations in which

---

19   Rachel Burger, interview.
20   Francis Bridger, typed dateline, ca. 1996.

they had been denied control; to recapitulate that with organizational control was absolutely against the guiding principles. Yet it was clear from the start that creating a context that was safe and nurturing meant, first of all, that women keep the location secret, and second, that they behave in a manner not threatening to other residents. At first, the belief was that the guests could devise rules as needed, with the exception of the one basic requirement: that the location of the house be kept secret. Over time, the group modified this approach, so the rules were not constantly shifting as the population of the shelter changed.

The staff (still mostly volunteers) tried to screen for severe mental illnesses and addictions and refer those affected women elsewhere. On a phone interview, however, screening was not always successful. Gradually, staff created rules about drinking and drug use, as well as rules about non-violence, particularly with respect to children. A resident who came to the shelter in 1980 remembers that there were about six rules.

Inevitably, there were crises. One woman told her husband where she was; another woman drank too much; there was a fight between two women where a knife was pulled. If only volunteers were in the building when a crisis arose, someone on the paid staff was called. Occasionally, a woman was asked to leave permanently, especially if her behavior threatened the security of the shelter. There was a short list of those who were not allowed to come back.

By 1978 five paid part-time employees and about 80 volunteers ran the house. The paid staff oversaw the work and did the jobs no one else wanted to do. Because of the large volunteer base, the existence of Transition House—but not its location—was well known in the community. The paid staff and all volunteers who were able to come participated in the weekly staff meetings. A smaller group of the most committed volunteers and paid staff made up the "core collective."

Roles were, by intention, fluid. "There were no boundaries," recalled one woman. The sense of excitement was tied to the strong sense of the power of sisterhood. Friendships and continuing relationships among staff and former guests were common. The husband of one staff person taught a former guest how to drive. A staff person babysat for the children of another former guest. One long-term volunteer still maintains contact with the grandchildren of a 1980s shelter guest.

In the beginning everyone did everything, and was "on call day and night." Increasingly, paid staff had specific responsibilities. Fund-raising became a specific job in the first years, and child-care specialist and volunteer coordinator positions were created. In 1979 a weekend staff person was hired, because too few volunteers wanted to work weekends.[21] Starting in 1980 volunteers were required to have some supervision from paid staff.[22] (Later, supervisors were sometimes senior volunteers, as knowledge and skill were not necessarily related to pay status.)

In January 1978, Transition House became an organization independent of the Women's Center. Articles of Organization were drafted and filed by Katherine Triantafillou. Incorporators were: Rachel Burger, president; Judith Moore, vice president; Cindy Bridger, treasurer; Judy Norris, clerk; and two more. The job titles were created to comply with the law, while the group actually continued to function as a collective. One of the key collective members from that period explained it to me: "the public face [of Transition House] was very conventional. We had a president in case we had to trot her out; had an annual meeting; jumped through the hoops of being a corporation. No one outside knew we were a collective. No one needed to know."

Many feminist organizations started as collectives. Collective governance represented an embracing of sisterhood and rejection of hierarchical [patriarchal] organization that was often disempowering and alienating to those lower in the hierarchy—disproportionally women and non-dominant group members. For a domestic violence shelter, it was also important that the women seeking shelter feel the power to manage their own lives, a power that had been denied them not only by societal privileging of men, but specifically by their abusive partners. Chris explained, "We chose to operate as a collective because we believe that we were not any better than anybody else and that everybody had a lot of valuable input to contribute to the organization."[23] It was the collective's aim that all the women—volunteers, staff and, guests—have an equal voice. In reality, few guests participated in collective meetings, although they had their own daily meetings.

It was volunteers and staff who fully embraced governing by collective. They were committed to hearing each person, to creating a context in which every woman could develop her own thinking and her own voice. The group talked through everything; the process was, indeed, empowering for many. Many interviewees reflected on their sense of power and shared ownership. For example: "We were accountable to each other. I have never had that work experience since." "I credit T House with formation of my understanding of

---

21   Francis Bridger, op cit.

22   Transition House newsletter, February 1980.

23   Chris Womendez. FMT, p. 10.

what women can do." "When it works, it is a glorious thing." "Because of the ownership people had in the structure and idea, all carried the vision into their lives and into the community."

Those in the core collective were aware that they were not only running a shelter, but were also a model for how the work should be done and for what it meant to be a feminist organization. Transition House was a leader in the movement. One woman remarked, "It wasn't just this shelter sheltering women and kids. There was the enormous impact T House had on how people think about domestic violence across so many sectors."[24] Although one of the early members felt "we were just a group of women running the shelter, and that worked out fine," most of those with whom I spoke acknowledged the presence of more complicated agendas, issues, and tensions from the beginning.

Some volunteers worked at Transition House for many years. Most, however, had shorter stays. As volunteers/staff came and went, changing the membership of the meetings, many issues were constantly revisited. One of the founding group reflected on the resulting tension: "You had to balance those who are holding the institution and the input of those who come through and won't stay." The reality that those with the biggest commitment to the house (over time and each week) actually did have more power was a problem. Either the ideal of complete equality of power had explicitly to be compromised, or those with more power risked resentment. Transition House held to the ideal, which did not fully match the reality. The founder of another shelter, who was trained by Transition House in the 1970s, said, "The collective model relies on the strength of particular people with power to get things to happen. The pretense is that there are no such people, but there always are. If they are good people, it works—until they leave. If personal power is used in negative ways, it is hierarchical, but hidden."[25]

Those who were "holding the institution" were in a difficult position. One staff person, looking back on those years, called the unwillingness to recognize individual contributions "[the] first great lesson in unintended consequences … It was hard for strong women to be their full strong selves. Most who brought that kind of strength could not stay." Almost everyone acknowledged that the collective process was extremely time-demanding and inefficient. Some volunteers and staff left because the lack of structure was too frustrating for them. The meetings were very long; they were also very intense.

---

24   Gail Sullivan, interview.

25   Robin Braverman, interview.

The collective was not only running a shelter and serving as a model for developing shelters, it was also a consciousness-raising group. "People were," as one participant observed, "working out what it means to be a radical feminist." Lesbian-identified women were important in the movement and also among the staff of Transition House. Homophobia was an issue for some of the individual guests, but it did not seem to be much of an issue within the collective. More difficult for the collective were issues of race and class, which the members were determined to address. These difficult conversations were new for most people, not only those at Transition House. There was a group for white women working on the issue of racism; a group of straight women looking at homophobia; and a support group for women in the collective who were living with men. A critique of patriarchy, suspicion of the institution of marriage, and focus on the power of women apart from men created obvious dilemmas for the (relatively few) married women in the collective. As one of them said: "Some of us were married. That was difficult, too. We formed our own support group ... It was hard for our husbands to keep up."

While the founders were women on welfare, by 1978 the collective was composed mostly of women from middle-class or privileged backgrounds, and mostly white. If they were themselves from working-class backgrounds, they were upwardly mobile. Many were college students. Collective members who were people of color or working-class-identified sometimes experienced their more privileged colleagues as entitled. It was difficult to talk about that in ways that were not hurtful. As those from more privileged backgrounds began to see their own assumptions, they were also hard on themselves and each other. They strove to be honest and to adhere to ideals of inclusiveness, equality, and sisterhood. The process generated powerful learning experiences and intensity among the relationships. At the same time, without intending to do so, "we created the opportunity to hurt each other."

One staff person from that time estimated the budget in 1978 was about $150,000. In the first years most of the money was raised by volunteers through personal solicitations. One staff person said, "We did all the things non-profits do; sent letters to everyone we knew, and they sent a few dollars." Artists among the staff created beautiful cards (Figure 2 is one of them), and handwritten requests were sent to tens of thousands of people, with whom volunteers had contact. Rachel remembered, "I illustrated holiday cards every year, which brought in [a lot of money] each year. A very touching thing about T House history was our carefully nurtured mailing list. Many former battered women and other poor women would send us as little as $5.00 a month. This is how we paid the rent for the first house on Elm Street."[26] Betsy's posters and Rachel's paintings were also sold to make money. Some volunteers were themselves wealthy (a fact they were likely not to mention), and may have been "stealth donors."

One volunteer who had been involved in the early days when the shelter operated in the apartment but had felt unwelcome as "too bourgeois," was asked to come back and help with funding. She wrote a proposal for CETA[27] money requesting $10,000 for a "social worker." That grant marked Transition House's first government funding and served as an early illustration of the tension between funders' ideas and expectations, and knowledge "on the ground." Mental health professionals had a (deserved) very bad reputation in the movement, and the collective had no intention of hiring a social worker. The money was really to be shared among a number of part-time positions. As was often the case at that time, Transition House protected its values, convictions, and nontraditional collective structure by misrepresenting itself to funders. Basically, the core distributed money wherever it was most needed at the time.

The volunteer group was largely white; the guests were more diverse, but also, at first, predominately white. Aware that they needed more diversity in the core group to achieve their ideals of inclusiveness, the collective recruited as a volunteer a Cambridge resident who was part of an African-American women's collective in the Boston area. Renae Gray started shortly after the move to the new house and then was hired with part of the CETA grant. Her job was both to reach out to women of color (then sometimes referred to as Third World women) and to help the white staff see what kept people of color from feeling more welcome. Cultural differences of race, class, and ethnicity (often overlapping) informed deep attitudes on many aspects of living in the house. White staff were encouraged to recognize their implicit cultural biases; for instance, in norms for self-expression, noise level, and child discipline.

Leadership in the Battered Women's Movement

People involved with Transition House were communicating with allies on many levels: with their own supporters locally; with people involved with the women's movement, nationally and internationally; and with those in what was now known as the "battered women's movement." Starting in 1978 and

---

26 Rachel Burger, interview.

27 The Comprehensive Employment and Training Act was a federal law (1973 to 1982) designed to train and provide jobs in public service for low-income and unemployed workers.

continuing with some interruptions until 2007, Transition House published an occasional newsletter. The newsletter reported on recent accomplishments; relevant city, state, and federal initiatives, including new laws and programs; new or impending cuts in funding for programs serving the women who stayed at the house; and (often) pleas for donations and for post-shelter housing. The newsletter appears to have been intended primarily to keep supporters informed and involved.

During the first year in the new house, staff hired a local filmmaker to make a documentary. The purpose of the film was to convey the story of Transition House, primarily for training volunteers and informing those who were starting shelters elsewhere. The filmmaker interviewed residents, volunteers and staff, and filmed people having informal conversations. Every few weeks the entire collective group looked at what she had shot and discussed it. Although, as the filmmaker noted in her interview, "editing by committee has no end," the group managed to get through the process, and in 1979 the collective produced a film, *We Will Not Be Beaten*, that was then lent to and viewed by many other groups. Viewing the documentary became part of the Transition House training and of the movement-building process; it was borrowed or rented by someone almost every day.

In 1978 Transition House participated in a national women's conference in Houston, at which a caucus on battered women advocated regional and national coalitions. Reporting on this conference, a participant wrote: "As a body, we were concerned with avoiding the experience of the anti-rape movement, whereby federal monies appropriated for services to rape victims were channeled into non-feminist professional service agencies rather than the grassroots groups whose years of unpaid work had provided initial service models and brought the problem to public attention in the first place."[28] Staff participated in Boston-area-wide meetings of women from local "alternative services run by and for women."[29] These included: Rosie's Place, Women, Inc., RESPOND, Casa Myrna Vasquez, Shelter Inc., and Columbia Point Alcoholism Project.

Most of the women who came to Transition House had legal issues. Katherine Triantafillou, a young feminist lawyer in Cambridge, became the Transition House legal advisor. Katherine had graduated from law school in 1975. When clients came to her who were dealing with battering issues, she contacted Betsy, whose aforementioned *Battered Women's Directory* was a preeminent

---

28   Transition House newsletter, early 1978, handwritten date, year only.

29   Transition House newsletter, June 1978.

resource. Soon, she reported, "I was essentially running a 24/7 legal hotline for women from T House."

Realizing some of the help did not require an actual lawyer, the group obtained a grant to support training advocates on relevant legal matters. These included understanding housing issues, drafting affidavits, and filing motions. From July 1977 until December 1978 Transition House had a legal advocacy program operating out of Arlington Street Church, staffed by Katherine and a new law school graduate, Chris Butler. Katherine and Chris trained nine paralegals as well as Transition House volunteers.

The core collective continued to develop its training program for volunteers and staff. No one, except for guests seeking refuge, was permitted to enter the shelter unless she had gone through the training. That meant *no one*; Chris Butler was required to take the training before being allowed into the shelter to talk to the women there about their legal issues. Training was intensive: three weekends over a three-week period. Because so many people volunteered at Transition House over the years the training itself became a significant movement-building activity.

Transition House guests interacted with many other agencies, and the staff tried to inform those agencies about the needs of domestic violence survivors. As part of their mission, one respondent said, "We were trying to change policies everywhere." For instance, the Welfare Department policy had not allowed checks to be mailed to US Post Office postal boxes, leaving survivors and their children without money while checks continued to be delivered to their former homes. A collaborative effort changed that policy. Staff alerted health care workers to the prevalence of domestic violence and gave them resources for referral; T House staff also identified a few key allies among pediatricians. In 1977 Katherine and Lisa began a project to train police. They encouraged the officers to carry pamphlets explaining resources for women dealing with violence, but found themselves frustrated with that effort and the considerable resistance of many officers.

Feminists in other communities who were hoping to open their own shelters looked to Transition House for guidance. Some local groups came to the trainings in Cambridge. As a founder of another shelter noted, "Transition House was the Mother of the Domestic Violence Movement in Massachusetts." In addition, Transition House volunteers and staff travelled all over the country to help other women's groups start shelters.

Telling the story from a national perspective, Susan Schechter referred to women from Transition House and Women's Advocates as "catalysts" for state, regional, and national coalitions. She wrote, "Through their struggle to define a 'feminist' shelter they gave birth to one more alternative, democratic women's institution. Although their efforts and ideology were not always replicated in other cities, Transition House and Women's Advocates became respected and often copied pioneers."[30]

As efforts to work with police seemed unsuccessful, Katherine and others from Transition House formed the Battered Women's Action Committee and drafted the Abuse Prevention Act. The Massachusetts legislature passed the act into law in 1978, as Massachusetts General Law 209A. The law provided protective orders for battered women and outlined police responsibility in situations of domestic violence. Women could now use the courts to apply for temporary and permanent restraining orders. Those involved felt "euphoric" when the law passed. One committee member captured the feeling: "We were a community of women changing society." Transition House training was expanded to include skill at applying for restraining orders. (Figure 3: Guide to APA.)

The programs at Transition House and RESPOND were receiving calls from men trying to find their sheltered partners and wanted a place to refer those men. Some women staying in the shelter or attending RESPOND's groups were hoping for their partners to get help. At the same time, men at the Boston Men's Center, which started in 1975 in Somerville, were learning about "battered women" from friends who were starting RESPOND and Transition House. Among those men was David Adams, a relatively recent college graduate who had known abuse in his family of origin. In response to the perceived need for a place at which the partners of battered women could get help, David joined with a small group to study how they might work with men who battered. They had bi-monthly meetings with key Transition House and RESPOND people, who also put them in touch with some of the women staying at the shelter and using the programs. One woman convinced her estranged husband to record his reflections on the battering. This gave David and his colleagues some insight into the ways, according to David, these men "romanticized, rationalized, and excused" their behavior.

Emerge, one of the early feminist-informed batterer programs, grew out of those conversations and opened in 1978 in Boston's Copley Square, where it stayed until moving to Cambridge in 1988. The battered women's movement—particularly the writing of Betsy Warrior and Lisa Leghorn—shaped Emerge's philosophy. For the first few years, referrals came from women at

---

30   Schechter, S. (1982). Op cit, p. 68.

**A WOMAN'S
GUIDE
to the
ABUSE
PREVENTION
ACT**

Figure 3: Guide to APA

the local shelters. Court referrals started in the early 1980s. Emerge became a partner with Transition House in movement-building activities, such as marches, training, and public speaking.

In 1978 eleven Massachusetts programs for battered women formed the Massachusetts Coalition of Battered Women Service Groups (The Coalition). The promise of government money spurred their partnership. Gail Sullivan explained: "The Massachusetts legislature was about to pass a law providing the first state funding for battered women services, and the grassroots feminist groups saw a coalition as a mechanism to avoid competing with each other and to strengthen their collective position to receive the funding."[31]

Although many of the 60 women who met to form The Coalition had participated in other meetings together, this collaborative effort revealed underlying differences in organizational politics and culture, which came as a surprise to many involved. For example, Casa Myrna Vasquez, coming out of a community of color, seemed more open to men as allies and to women survivors maintaining ties with their families. Transition House was seen as a movement leader, and also more radical than others. As a result of such differences among programs, some of the meetings were painful, as the group tried to create common key principles. Nonetheless, they got the funding. Gail asserted, "By the time the state issued the request for proposals, we had helped shape the focus of the funding, and coalition member groups were in a good position to get it."[32]

The Coalition became, then, the umbrella organization for the grassroots shelters and programs. Many of its founding staff came from Transition House. One of the lawyers who had worked with Transition House was hired in 1979 to train advocates; one of the Transition House staff who had been among the initiators of The Coalition was hired as full-time staff there. In December 1979, Congress passed H.R. 2977, the Domestic Violence Prevention and Services Act. This would allow federal support for the National Council on Domestic Violence and the Massachusetts Coalition, among others.[33]

Conclusion

The Transition House pioneers had accomplished an astounding amount in just a few years. By the end of the 1970s a functioning domestic violence

---

31 Sullivan, G. (1981). *For Shelter and Beyond, First Edition*. "The Movement Against Woman Abuse." Massachusetts Coalition of Battered Women Service Groups. p. 19.

32 Sullivan, G. interview.

33 Transition House newsletter, February 1980.

shelter existed in Cambridge in its own house and served as a model for new shelters elsewhere. Its staff was figuring out how to run a shelter consistent with feminist principles. The group that organized and ran the house was in the forefront of changes being made all over the country. A state coalition was active; a local group for men who battered was up and running; a new state law created the option of protective orders for domestic violence victims; new federal legislation was enacted; training materials were developed that were widely used and copied.

Perhaps it is not surprising that many of the most active movement builders and Transition House leaders were exhausted and felt they needed time to heal. The work ethic was not sustainable. As one of them said, "everyone was over-extended …. and took pride in that." In addition, there was as yet no recognition of the effect on caregivers of constant exposure to crises and trauma. Also, the experience of women in conflict with each other in the movement and in the organization itself was, for some, profoundly disillusioning. Among the pioneers who left, some sought perspective and healing in a spiritual path and practice. Some continued to work on women's issues elsewhere; others shifted their energy to other movements or began to establish more traditional careers.

Transition House was founded as a social change organization and was running a shelter with allied programs serving those affected by domestic violence. Tension between the founding missions of social change and social service would continue to be an important theme throughout the following decades.

CHAPTER 2

1980s Building and Expanding, New Programs and New Challenges

The Changing Context

The efforts of the 1970s had created greatly increased awareness of domestic violence on city, state, and national levels. Many legal, social services, and health agencies had at least some training on domestic violence; more public money was available; and there were laws and policies intended to benefit battered women. Nonetheless, Transition House still held a profound distrust of establishment institutions.

While the 1970s were the pioneering and movement-building years, the 1980s are harder to characterize. Transition House continued to develop path-breaking programs, train large numbers of volunteers and staff, shelter abused women, and counsel women on the phone. An outstanding initiative during this decade was the Dating Violence Intervention Project (DVIP), started in 1985. This prevention project, aimed at high school and middle school students, grew through the 1980s and 1990s as an important part of Transition House and a model for programs throughout the country. Meanwhile, as this project was being developed, Transition House faced new challenges that reflected those the entire country was confronting.

As the policies of the Reagan years took effect, it became more difficult for people to escape poverty. Safety net programs were being cut, and housing in the greater-Boston area was becoming increasingly expensive. As it was harder for women to find housing, shelter stays got longer. The woman who headed the Cambridge Women's Commission in the 1980s put it succinctly: "The world became so difficult." During the 1980s it became more common to find women at Transition House for whom the most pressing issue was homelessness, rather than domestic violence. In a stunning incident, one such woman snuck her husband into the shelter.

Staff members were also becoming more aware of the complexities of intimate violence. "It had not occurred to us," said one of the early group, "that women would go back [to their abusers]." The staff was also becoming aware of battering in lesbian relationships. One respondent said, "In some ways we had a simplistic analysis when we started." She tellingly added: "Maybe that helped."

The Shelter and The Collective

Transition House celebrated its 5th birthday in 1981 with a party at, and co-sponsored by, the Cambridge YWCA. At the event, the film *We Will Not Be Beaten* was shown continuously. In the newsletter for June 1981, Transition House announced the celebration and proclaimed: "We've gone from an overflowing apartment to a 22-room house, and our work is constantly expanding and improving." The poster created for the 5th birthday emphasizes women uniting across differences: "Unless we're united, Black, white, yellow, or any color, rich or poor; unless we're united, this problem is going to continue from generation to generation; our daughters, our granddaughters will have to deal with this problem…so we have to unite as much as we can." (Figure 4: "Unless We're United.")

At that time, about 45 women and children were staying at the shelter each month. Liz's story gives details of one woman's experience at Transition House in the early 1980s. Liz came to Transition House in April of 1980 with her sons, ages 6 and 2. She describes the events that led her to Transition House, and her experience there:

> I met my husband when I was 14. He was from the Middle East. We met in Harvard Square. My older sisters hung out there, and I met him through them. At 15 I was pregnant. I came from an Irish-Catholic family in Dorchester, and my family was not pleased. I also got pretty much thrown out of high school. I got my GED. I was married when I was 17 (1974). He was abusive even before that. I thought this meant he loved me.
>
> With my best friend I went to the Women's School at the Women's Center for a self- defense class. There I met a T House volunteer. That night I went to a lesbian bar— everyone was going there. I felt safe there. When I got home my husband beat the crap out of me with the kids in the room. I called T House, but they were full. I called

(Figure 4: "Unless We're United.")

another shelter, but couldn't stay there because I lived in that town. When I called T House again, they said I could stay if I was willing to sleep in the children's room. For the first night we slept there and then got a room. We had mattresses on the floor. No doors (inside the house) were locked. There was a wheel on the fridge for which night you cooked. It was such a collective, both staff and residents.

I stayed for six weeks or more. I love T House. It saved my life; mine and my kids'. They still remember where it is, and they have never told anyone.

I started learning about feminism. I went to the collective meetings. Some other residents did not usually seem to care. They just wanted a safe place to stay and then to move on. At night the residents would talk about "never again" and how we would raise our daughters or nieces differently. There was no staff at night. I'd sleep in the staff room and answer the hotline. We were smoking and drinking. We'd sneak it in.

The kids loved the child care. They loved the house. One of my best friends to this day was a staff member there. I came out there. I would go out to lesbian clubs with the staff, went to a staff person's house for dinner. There wasn't any separation of staff and clients. The staff embraced me. I didn't feel like I was any different. We were going out at night and dancing together.

I did public speaking for T House. I felt like I had a voice for the first time, especially when I was doing public speaking. After I left T House, I came back and volunteered on the hotline and did public speaking for many years.

When I left T House I lived with a friend who had also left her abusive husband and had two sons. I stayed there for nine months then moved in with staff from T house. We are still friends to this day; she had a son the same age as my youngest. We raised our kids together. I supported myself with low-paying jobs, driving people around and odd jobs. I ended up homeless myself at one point in 1983, and my kids stayed with family. I lived in a VW bug for a while.

He [her ex-husband] was always after me. The kids had visits ordered by the court. We were in court a lot. He still abused me until he finally committed suicide in 1987. I had started on a Bachelor in Social Work degree. I stopped when my ex-husband killed himself, and the kids were still pretty young. Obviously, it was an upsetting time, and they needed me. I started again when my younger son was in college.

In the late 1980s (when in college) I returned to T House to do over-nights, until the shelter had to be temporarily closed because of mice. The building was in really bad shape. And it seemed less political. There were more rules. I think if there had been a lot of rules when I stayed there I might have left. I eventually got a job working with homeless kids and started my work in human services.

I also had an abusive relationship with a woman. Because she was a woman I kept thinking she was going to get it and would stop. This time, the abusive partner was the one who had to leave. My husband was from another culture, but that does not explain the violence. His brother married my close friend and is not at all violent. Plenty of US-born men are violent.

I still think T House is an incredible place that saves people's lives. At the same time, I feel sad. Domestic violence still happens. People still say the same things—why did she stay? The other person is not always bad. My husband had some good and endearing qualities. When you leave you lose everything. I still miss some of the things I left behind, things my parents gave me when I was a child. I had missed my teddy bear, but I knew it was gone, because the kids saw him destroy it.[34]

When Liz stayed at T House in 1980, the expected length of stay was still four weeks for single women, and six weeks for women with children. From today's perspective, when a 12-week limit has been abandoned as inadequate, this seems a very short time. In 1980, however, it seemed long enough to warrant justification in the welcome sheet: "We feel women often need this much time to restructure their lives—but those who have gained enough support from the house may be directed to overflow before their limit is up, as we are

---

34   Paraphrased from an interview with Liz and reviewed by her for inclusion here.

continually filled to capacity."[35]

In the early 1980s, Transition House's population represented women from many cultural and ethnic groups. Most of them were poor, and many had not had paid employment. With help from the staff they needed to secure public welfare assistance; enroll the children in Cambridge schools; handle legal and court-related issues, which included custody issues; and address their own health and wellness. Some women had avoided seeking medical care because they were ashamed of bruises or other evidence of beatings. A housing advocate helped them begin the search for housing.

During the 1980s Lee Ann Hoff, a doctoral student, volunteered and did "collaborative research" at Transition House, producing a book in 1990 titled *Battered Women as Survivors*.[36] A short section gives another window into the experience of residents later in the 1980s. Based on "good-bye interviews" with women leaving the shelter, Lee Ann states that "Most evaluated their experience as very good, and provided specific comments about the positive aspects of their experience there." Some of the residents' comments follow:

- "There was always someone to talk to—staff or another woman …"
- "It's excellent places like this exist. The staff are very liberal and let women lead their own life and give information when needed. I feel kind of let down on some things, but I got stronger … No man will run my life anymore."
- "Support from other women. The staff are really good, especially at listening and letting you be yourself. I could be myself. I didn't have that with my husband."
- "A roof over my head, security. It was a fighting experience, fighting for myself and my children to think positive."[37]

Lee Ann goes on to say, "The one persistent criticism concerned the bickering and petty conflicts among the residents themselves, and the residents' perception that the staff [was] not able to intervene effectively in these conflicts. They also complained about 'too many meetings,' overcrowding, dirt, a 'rat in my room,' not enough linens, and 'kids running around the house.'"[38]

Friction among the women and outbursts against children were not rare, but weekends seemed particularly fraught. By Friday night, the residents' tension

---

35 Welcome sheet, 1980, p.1.

36 Hoff, L. (1990). *Battered Women as Survivors*. London: Routledge.

37 Hoff, L. (1990). Op cit, pp. 153-154.

38 Op cit, p.154.

and anxiety sometimes reached a tipping point, and those volunteering on weekends worked to keep the house peaceful without violating the dignity and autonomy of the residents. One volunteer explained, "We were big on empowerment. That was the word we used all the time. We didn't want to be bossy, like the batterer was. [We'd say something like], 'You work with me now to figure out what you can do. You cannot hit the kid. Put yourself in the kid's place. You know what that is like.'"

Rules for the women staying at the shelter continued to be an area of struggle. When something happened that staff or resident women did not like, the staff would often respond by creating a new rule, which the residents often supported. However, the rules were difficult to enforce, especially with a philosophy of equal power to all. Boundaries between those staying at T House and those working there were very fluid. Residents wrote in the logs and read the logs. When rules were broken, the staff experienced tension between feeling empathy and setting limits. It was difficult to be consistent.

Transition House had been a leader in developing a structured child-care program in a shelter, including foster grandparents for some children and parenting support for mothers. The staff started a children's caucus at The Coalition in the mid-1980s to share their knowledge and experience with the other shelters and programs in the state.[39]

Transition House established a new savings incentive program in 1982. Federal cuts in welfare and Women, Infants, and Children (WIC) benefits, food stamps, and housing support had a deeply negative effect on the women staying at the shelter. The savings program was partly a response to the increased difficulty women faced in finding housing and managing financially. The staff, through the savings incentive program, gave women $15 for every $100 they saved for housing while at Transition House.[40]

Starting in 1983 a new telephone exchange coordinated seven shelters to locate available beds. This was a resource for the volunteer on the hotline. As before, some calls led to a woman coming to the shelter or being referred to another shelter, but most did not. One former volunteer reported: "The calls tended to be long—usually one or two a night. Sometimes callers knew what they needed, asked for help, and I had a book of resources. Those were fairly quick. More often the woman was stuck, her partner was out. They just wanted to talk, were not ready for action. You could hear in the women's voices that

---

39 Transition House newsletter, Spring 1987.
40 Transition House newsletter, November 1982.

they felt helped by talking to someone."

Deeply committed to the principle of all members running the house, and undeniably aware of the difficulty of that process, the staff forged a compromise in the late 1980s. Partly in response to funders' pressure, Transition House constructed its version of a board of directors.

The bylaws for 1988 state: "The Board of Directors shall be known as the Coordinating Committee (the CORE) and shall consist of ten designated volunteers, all full-time paid staff members, and all active members of the Corporation." Active members of the Corporation included: "volunteers and paid staff who have satisfactorily completed Volunteer Training [and] residents of Transition House living at the shelter."[41] The CORE was to be responsible for general management, and any changes in overall program plan or philosophy had to be brought before CORE. Ten volunteers were selected each year to participate in the CORE; but the bylaws suggest, at the same time, that everyone could still participate in decision making. The ambiguity signifies T House's strong reluctance to delegate power to a smaller group, even as they were explicitly doing so.

The day-to-day business of the house was still run by volunteers and staff, each of whom was part of, and responsible to, a committee. The increased number and complex assignments of these committees reflect the growth in the organization. Standing committees were: In-House (including maintenance), volunteer task force (including community support groups and volunteer training), child support, parenting support, advocacy/family. The CORE was in charge of outreach and education, participation in The Coalition, T House films, policy, finance, hiring and ad hoc.[42]

The weekly meetings of the 1980s were described similarly to those of the 1970s. One staff member, a person of color, captured many people's sense of both empowerment and frustration: "I came from the corporate world. I felt empowered. I had a voice, and people would listen. For me, being an oppressed person, to be in an organization where people would listen to me— it was great. I felt equal to the rest of the staff. [But] it took a long time to get things done. A lot of personality, a lot of emotion, crying, people walking out."

As in the earlier years of Transition House, there were some who had no patience with the collective process. One volunteer admitted, "[It] drove me nuts … pointlessly long discussions over minutia of household supplies.

---

41 Bylaws for 1988, pp. 2 and 3.

42 *Transition House Training Manual: Part 1*, late 1980s.

Women who worked there were deeply committed to the process and wanted all voices to be heard. I thought that was ridiculous, that my voice should carry as much weight." Similarly, from another volunteer, "I was uncomfortable with anarchy, and the culture of the organization reinforced it …We were going to keep repeating the same problems over and over as new people came in." Those who were alienated by the process often did not stay long. For many who did stay, they formed lifelong bonds with their colleagues. One volunteer said, "People who worked at T House with me are the closest thing to an old boy network."

The newsletter for June 1981 includes the usual plea for donations, still Transition House's most important source of support, supplemented by grants and state money. State money came to all the battered women shelters and programs through the Department of Social Services (DSS). Finances, however, were always inadequate. Fear of impending cuts in state money for social services (an implicit acknowledgement of Transition House's having moved, at least to some extent, into that category) increased the urgency for fund-raising.

United Way, another possible source of funds, presented some challenges; specifically, the non-profit organization required a site visit before a grant could be made, which Transition House would not allow. Also, some feared that funds received from United Way would compromise the organization's politics and demand a different structure. One respondent expressed the ambivalence well: "It grieved me. I loved the revolutionary egalitarian scene, but knew it couldn't survive. We already had CETA grants and welfare [DSS] money. I don't want to see it, but know it has to happen." Ultimately, the group members decided to give it a try—on their own negotiated terms.

Transition House people convinced United Way representatives to meet them at the Women's Center, not the shelter. They appointed the one staff person who had an MBA to present the proposal, in hopes that her business degree and style would impress the United Way representatives enough for them to accept the unorthodox collective structure. Indeed, she simply declared: "That is the structure, and it works." Transition House received its first United Way funds in 1982.

The next year, however, United Way insisted on seeing the shelter. To fund a facility that they could not visit was too much to expect of that funding organization. Finally, the two groups reached a compromise. United Way agreed to give support if staff members could visit the shelter once. They also agreed for their representatives to be picked up in a designated location and blindfolded for the trip to the shelter. At the appointed time, a T House staff person met them. "I drove them in circles, three of them," the driver told me. The blindfolds came off in the shelter and went back on for a return trip of detours to the drop-off spot.

In a meeting the following year, in spite of their earlier agreement to visit the shelter only once, United Way representatives again insisted on a site visit. The same person who did the driving the prior year reported: "They swore it would be a one-time thing. Then the next year they wanted to come back. I yelled at them." She was, she acknowledges, playing "bad cop." Although she was really angry, those involved knew they were not going to refuse United Way's ongoing support.

The story of the blindfolded funders became an important part of the oral history of Transition House. It seems to mark a turning point between the determined self-sufficiency of the founding years and the social service status of the later years. United Way representatives recognized the organization's importance and wanted to be involved, or they would not have put up with the indignities to which they were subjected. Transition House people believed that T House was reaching the limit of its ability to expand without more help from the world of established social services, or they would not have risked their independence.

The founding philosophy of Transition House was women helping women, anti-social service, anti-establishment. As one of the pioneers, who stayed through the 1980s, said: "We were pushing hard against a social service model. There was pressure to hire a social worker or mental health people. We hired mostly former battered women and people with a feminist orientation." According to another, the staff still felt "we are crusaders … it is us against the world." At the same time, new relations with DSS and United Way forced Transition House to account for its work to outside agencies. In the 1980s federal funds also became available through the Family Violence Prevention and Services Act passed in 1984. In the early years, some misrepresentation on reports to protect clients' confidentiality or maintain Transition House's political integrity seemed warranted. As government and mainstream agencies got more involved, avoiding outside oversight became more difficult.

By the end of the decade about 80 families a year were staying at the shelter.[43] In 1989 state budget cuts meant all the shelters would lose needed funds. The organizations with larger budgets (of which Transition House was one) agreed to put some dollars into the collective pot for other shelters to share.

---

43 Transition House newsletter, December 1989.

Transition House continued to send out its personal holiday pleas for money, each one an artist-created card.

Almost all those who had started the shelter and worked there in the 1970s had left by 1984. New volunteers were constantly being trained. Many of this new group stayed as volunteers, staff and (later) board members for decades. T House became a central part of their lives; and they were absolutely essential to the continuity and survival of the organization through the 1980s and most of the 1990s.

By the mid-1980s T House included paid staff, volunteer staff, work-study students and interns, temporary paid staff and consultants, as well as people paid from a grant or special program. Special programs included foster grandparents and Commonwealth Service Corps members.[44] All paid staff and volunteers were required to participate in the intensive training, and paid staff had an additional requirement to attend at least three relevant trainings, conferences, or workshops per year. Interns had a shorter required training and were encouraged also to participate in the longer one.

Paid staff and volunteers experienced tension between their groups. Paid staff members worked in offices downstairs, less intimately connected with the residents. The volunteers, upstairs, felt as if they, themselves, were running the shelter and were not sure those downstairs even knew all their names. They also sometimes felt they knew better what was needed. They were more inclined to bend rules to fit a guest's needs; for instance, extending a length of stay. They were also more in touch with the issues of drug and alcohol misuse in the house. The paid staff members were slightly older and had been involved longer. There was also some tension between people with a movement history and those who saw their work at the shelter more as a job. One person who volunteered while in college in the 1980s captured this divide: "T House staff felt part of a movement. My generation didn't feel like part of a movement because of earlier successes."

It was becoming clear to some that Transition House's traditional informality and flexibility of roles, looseness of boundaries, and assumption that each person would give her all to the organization did not fit the current situation and realities. Without official policies governing staff, it was impossible to hold people accountable for lapses in their work, and there were lapses. What was best for the organization was not necessarily best for the individual, and sometimes the organization's interests were not put first. In one unusually dramatic situation, two staff members had been drinking alcohol while

---

44   Transition House personnel policies, undated ca. 1986, np.

on the job, and it was difficult for other staff people to confront them and address it. It seemed necessary to create a more official job structure, and a committee went to work on writing personnel policies.

The organizational ethic had been one of sisterhood, mutual trust, and common purpose, against hierarchy and official rules. The personnel policy manual of the mid-1980s, like the story of the blindfolded funders, exemplifies the tension between the politics and principles of the early years and the realities of the mid-1980s.

A section of the manual states: "One of the most important staff benefits at Transition House is that we function as a collective and not within a hierarchy. Each staff member is responsible for the whole collective. Decisions are made at weekly staff meetings, at quarterly CORE meetings, and at monthly potlucks. All meetings (staff, potluck, CORE) are open to paid and volunteer staff alike."[45]

The same manual avers that paid staff must account for hours worked and have those hours verified by another staff person. Such a rule certainly suggests the ethos of collective responsibility was strained (at least). The manual even specifies the amount of break time per shift: "A fifteen minute break every four hours and one half hour break in each eight hour day." Guidelines for sick days, vacation days, and benefits were all spelled out in the policies. There was no way to avoid the fact that for many staff, this was now a job. At the same time, "Promotion procedures do not apply because Transition House is a non-hierarchical organization." And "Job descriptions and titles are meant to define individual staff members' specific responsibilities and in no way represent any kind of power designation." All staff were paid at the same rate: $28,000 per year.

The hiring section of the manual begins with affirmative action principles and states the "affirmative action goal is one-third staffing by lesbians, one-third staffing by women of color, one-half and no less than one-third staffing by former battered women." The second and third of these goals make perfect sense, given the philosophy of peer help. Many of the guests were women of color; they were all survivors of battering; therefore, the staff should also have women of color and formerly battered women. The goal for a significant lesbian presence is less obviously in service of the mission. Very few guests were lesbian-identified, but a high proportion of the early leaders of Transition House were. The influence of lesbian-identified women in the

---

45   Transition House personnel policies, undated ca. 1986, np, would be page 10.

larger movement and in Transition House was immense. For some, the ability and desire to live without men represented the epitome of women's liberation and empowerment. The inclusion of lesbians as one of the priority groups for hiring probably reflects the effort to keep empowerment of women as a central focus for the organization.

In the early 1980s six new paid staff were hired, four of them women of color. In 1989, for the first time, the leadership laid off some staff as a result of $24,000 in state budget cuts. All T House residents and staff protested at the Massachusetts State House. The budget woes continued into the 1990s.

The Movement

Transition House served as a model for other communities. A Transition House newsletter from 1982 reports that visitors from China, India, Bahamas, Singapore, and Pakistan came to learn about starting shelters or programs.[46] The DVIP became another exemplary program. In addition, T House was a major player in the statewide network of shelters and programs for battered women. Beyond those activities, movement building, which would require energy and time for meetings apart from the more immediate work of running the shelter, is less evident in the 1980s. Possibly The Coalition was seen as the focus for that work. Gail Sullivan, a former T House staffer, then at The Coalition, wrote in its publication, *For Shelter and Beyond*: "Our work is not simply to provide service, though that is itself an enormous task; we need to change attitudes, raise consciousness and take action ... We need to build coalitions with other groups, such as anti-rape groups, anti-racist groups and those working for reproductive rights, economic justice, child-care needs, etc."[47]

Training was an important part of the organization's work. Transition House trained hundreds of volunteers and staff over the years as well as women from other communities seeking to start their own programs. In addition, staff and former staff were major contributors to *For Shelter and Beyond*, which The Coalition published in 1981 to help groups across the state with training. T House, in turn, used articles from *For Shelter and Beyond*, as the T House training was continually revised.

Many who began as staff or volunteers in the 1980s spoke about the power of the training. Below are two examples:

---

46   Transition House newsletter, November 1982.

47   Sullivan, G. (1981). *For Shelter and Beyond, First Edition.* "Why a Coalition." p. 19. See also Allen, C. (1992, 1990). *For Shelter and Beyond, Second Edition.* "Coalition Building," p. 19.

This is really great. Because I was a woman who didn't feel empowered. We could do this. I can start incorporating this into my life.

I went to the training. It was mind-blowing. That training in itself basically changed my life … It opened my eyes to all the isms that I knew existed, but wasn't paying much attention to.

The *Transition House Training Manual, Part 1* from the late-1980s (undated) includes a section on outlook and philosophy, with a short history of the movement, and the Principles of Unity of Transition House. These principles of unity were at the forefront of the training and affirmed the organization's feminist foundation and anti-racist, -classist and -homophobic principles. In addition, statements in the document affirm that consciousness–raising was still part of the mission: "We will encourage women to see the connections between their experiences and those of other women whether battered or not, and to see the larger issues affecting their lives, such as sexism, racism, power relations in general. We'll encourage women in the House to learn about feminism and to get involved with the women's movement."[48] The principles of unity also reiterate: "We are committed to continuing to be a non-professional staff."[49]

Succeeding chapters in the training manual on working with battered women include: women of color; issues of class, legal, and welfare advocacy; mothers and mothering; women with other emotional issues; and supporting battered lesbians. Issues of race and class had been central concerns of Transition House from the start. The need to address both emotional issues and battered lesbians had become clear with experience and were in some tension with the stance against mental health treatment and the analysis in terms of patriarchal oppression.

In the early 1980s, the community outreach committee began working with the Emerge staff and developed a four-session prevention education curriculum for teens that was piloted at a Somerville youth program and subsequently funded by the Massachusetts Department of Health.[50, 51] In a few years this beginning grew into an innovative program, which became a model for other programs around the country and the basis for training teachers and police

---

48   Principles of Unity p. 3, in *Transition House Training Manual: Part 1,* nd, np.

49   Ibid, p. 4.

50   Transition House newsletter, November 1981.

51   Transition House newsletter, Spring 1983.

officers on preventing and responding to dating violence.

Carole Sousa, DVIP's long-time director, gave this testimony to a Congressional committee in 1993:

> In 1985 Transition House, a shelter for battered women and their children, gave shelter to two battered women who had been to the shelter ten years earlier as children with their battered moms. The shelter staff decided they didn't want to be part of a tradition of just sheltering generations of abused women. The lives of these two battered women, as well as increased numbers of hot line calls from teens and those who work with teens about dating violence, motivated the staff of Transition House to form the Dating Violence Intervention Project."[52]

Locally, Transition House was finding it difficult to work with the city due to the shelter's collective structure and its long-held suspicion of established institutions. In turn, those established institutions found it challenging to work with Transition House. Those responsible for Community Development Block Grants, which supported shelter services, had a hard time figuring out who at the organization was responsible or accountable. The fire department was never clear who was in charge when there was a fire alarm. Because women were sent to shelters outside of their own town, it was also difficult for Cambridge to see the benefits for its own community members. Cambridge had had a Women's Commission within the city government since 1977, and its new head in 1980 had previously been director of a domestic violence program in another city. From her perspective, the people at Transition House had a "bunker mentality." A natural ally, she felt frustrated by some of the barriers to collaborative work with T House. The stance of "us against the world" was beginning to be less rational and counterproductive as some of "the world" was now in a better position to be an ally.

The DVIP served, to a large degree, as Transition House's ambassador to the city of Cambridge. It had the advantages of being somewhat independent of the shelter and having excellent leadership. Being embedded in the schools, it necessarily involved collaboration with the city. During the latter 1980s DVIP was the part of Transition House that maintained the strongest relationship with the Cambridge community.

---

52   Testimony of Carole Sousa, Hearing of the US Senate Committee on Labor and Human Resources, July 1993.

Conclusion

Throughout the 1980s Transition House trained hundreds of new volunteers and staff, provided a safe refuge for hundreds of women and children, and continued to serve as a model for new programs in the United States and other countries. The children's program developed, and the DVIP became an innovative and successful prevention program for high school and middle school students.

In retrospect, and probably only in retrospect, we can see the contradictions with which Transition House dealt. The dramatic successes of the 1970s had created public awareness, which led to government funding for shelters and, thereby, a dilemma for an organization conceived as a social change organization and deeply suspicious of official institutions and oversight. This contradiction was embedded in The Coalition. Initiated by Transition House people, among others, it was a movement-sustaining organization created to get state money. The development of state and federal laws and funding related to domestic violence pulled T House (and other shelters and programs) away from their grassroots foundations.

Lisa Leghorn, who left before the 1980s, described the tension from her perspective in an interview:

> We never had the idea that we were a social service. We were raising consciousness about the relationship between women's unpaid labor and violence in the home, raising consciousness about violence against women in general. All those people who came did it for that reason, to empower women. The model was women supporting women, not trained social workers helping clients. But funders said—how do we support it long term? It's a service and should be paid for. So, who are we? A movement for social change or a social work organization?"

The women's movement, itself, was in a different stage. As the pioneers of Transition House moved on, new volunteers and staff varied in their commitment to the feminist founding principles of Transition House. At the same time, the organization grew in complexity. The collective governance had two primary purposes: to run the shelter and to raise consciousness. It had never been efficient, and in the 1980s it was increasingly problematic.

CHAPTER 3
1990s: Holding On and Letting Go

Transition House was 15 years old in 1991. As part of the celebration of that occasion, T House contracted two filmmakers to work with the staff on a second film about battered women and about Transition House, a modern update of *We Will Not Be Beaten*. The filmmakers spoke about the project at the time: "It not only documents the experience of women who have survived battering and gone on to change their lives, but also documents the battered women's movement. [It] is about looking at that history and bringing it to the present."[53] (Figure 5: 15th Anniversary.)

The filmmakers recorded hours of tape, and compiled one segment of the anticipated film for the collective to review. This time the collective could not agree on the specifics of what should be included and what should be excluded from the project. Everyone involved remembers differently what the disagreements were about; some remember only that there was a lot of conflict. At the last minute, after the booklet for the celebration, which was to include the film, was printed and a lot of money invested, the filmmakers could not make the film. The one segment that the collective reviewed was destroyed, and the original tapes were relegated to the shelter basement. Ironically, one of the filmmakers had praised the collective as "the most productive organization I've ever seen."[54]

It was increasingly difficult to live by the founding feminist principles, to which Transition House still held allegiance. The revolutionary fervor of the founding group and the excitement of a new movement had passed. The environment in which Transition House had originally existed had changed,

---

53   15-year celebration booklet, p. 14.
54   Ibid, p. 16.

(Figure 5: 15th Anniversary.)

partly as a result of the efforts of the earlier years of the battered women's movement, and partly as a result of national policies and market forces that made moving out of poverty much more difficult.

Many of those who joined the volunteers and staff in the 1980s stayed well into the 1990s and longer. This group managed to maintain or expand existing programs and develop important new initiatives while dealing with difficult challenges to, and ultimately changes in, the culture and structure of the organization.

External and Internal Challenges

Two external trends had profound effects on the internal working of T House and its programs. First, mainstream institutions were more involved with domestic violence issues and more informed, thanks largely to the efforts of T House leaders and others in the preceding decades. Secondly, economic trends and national policies contributed to increased difficulty in finding housing or economic viability for those who were homeless and unemployed.

Robin Braverman, who had founded another local shelter, described the first trend this way: "The institutions did change. So, it was possible to get help from them. The model does not have to be in opposition to them, as it used to be. We succeeded in changing the institutions so there *can* be a social service model. The negative part is the concept of women helping women is harder to find. The social service model loses women empowering themselves."

New funding streams, laws, and oversight brought benefits for domestic violence survivors and for Transition House. They also created some perverse incentives and challenged T House's culture and structure.

In 1991 the Massachusetts Abuse Prevention Act was amended, increasing police directives to arrest alleged offenders and restraining order violators. Massachusetts developed a Governor's Commission on Domestic Violence in 1992. About the same time, DSS, as a result of conflict with shelters and awareness that the mothers in its caseloads were often themselves battered, started a Domestic Violence Unit, staffed by people who were veterans of the early domestic violence programs. In 1994, Congress passed the Violence Against Women Act, with, among other provisions, federal funding of services for victims of rape and domestic violence. In 1997, the governor of Massachusetts issued an executive order stating "zero tolerance" for domestic violence. These changes, a product of the earlier work, created more funds and potentially more allies, in addition to increased oversight.

As state and national agencies developed their own sense of expertise on domestic violence issues, the deference to T House diminished. The most relevant case in point was the organization's primary funder. As one respondent put it, "We no longer had the upper hand with DSS." State involvement inadvertently created a system of incentives that resulted in some women using shelter for purposes other than finding safety. Women "savvy to the system" knew they could (at that time) get housing faster from a domestic violence shelter than from a homeless shelter, as survivors of domestic violence had special access to vouchers for housing. As residents, such women were more likely to breach security by calling a partner or giving out the location. This became a new screening issue. The child protection system, newly aware of the risks to children who witness violence, began responding to violence against a mother as a child protection issue. In the early 1990s a DSS worker might see a woman at an emergency room and threaten to remove her children if the woman did not go to shelter. In order to avoid that outcome, some women came to the shelter who were not really ready to leave their partners and were more likely to disregard rules.

With government funding and involvement, there was increased pressure on the movement organizations to professionalize. T House resisted this pressure. One respondent explained, "We are the professionals in this work. It does not imply a hierarchy. We are the leaders. [It's a] different definition of professional."[55] One Coalition board member started volunteering at T House in the early 1990s specifically because it appeared to be loyal to its movement roots—still a collective, after most collectives had ended, and still political.

The second trend, regressive changes in the country's policies, made the work of shelters much more difficult. Affordable housing was increasingly scarce due to national policies, market forces, and, locally, to the ending of rent control in the mid-1990s. Safety net services for the poor continued to be eroded. For more and more women who sought shelter, getting to a point of economic and housing security in four to six weeks was unrealistic. In addition, fewer hospital or community options existed for women with mental illness and/or addiction issues, which meant more women with serious problems in addition to homelessness and violence sought shelter at Transition House.

There were also internal challenges. Three issues particularly concerned the collective in the early 1990s: 1) how to address the homophobia of many of the guests; 2) how to combat the collective's own ongoing tensions concerning race; and 3) how to continue as a collective. Transition House hired Visions, a minority consulting group, to help. "They helped us talk out the struggle

---

55   VT13: Videotape, 1991, at approx. 21:10.

around race, explaining where people are coming from, why staff might have more problems with minority guests," reported one participant. They were not able to help solve ongoing problems with the collective. The collective was at this point limited to paid staff; the CORE, all volunteers, was to function like a board. The staff, however, believed that they themselves made the decisions. As one said, "That's how it really was." A member of the CORE reflected on this arrangement as "the worst of all worlds."

The shelter building, itself, was another challenge. It was greatly in need of repair and refurbishing, and rodents were a constant problem. Serious repair would require serious money. A plea to supporters and a grant from the city yielded enough to pour a new foundation, without shutting the shelter's doors.[56] Other repairs were deferred.

The two challenges that most dramatically represented change for Transition House were creating an effective governance structure and balancing the empowerment philosophy with a perceived need to provide professional services to women facing complicated challenges. In both areas, governance and the stance toward the residents, large gaps developed and grew between the expressed ideology of the collective and the organization's actual work with women and children in the shelter.

The Shelter and The Collective, Early 1990s

All shelters in The Coalition had earlier agreed that residents should not come from, or have intimate connections to, the town in which the shelter was located. In addition, no boys over age 12 were allowed in the shelters, in order to maintain the man-free space. Transition House did take on male volunteers as child caretakers to provide positive male role models, but these volunteers did not go upstairs to the residents' bedroom area. The effort to screen out women with serious mental health or drug issues had never been successful and was apparently abandoned.

By the early 1990s new screening criteria emerged for women seeking refuge. It is unclear when these new criteria were instituted. Screening attempted to limit residents to those who were seeking shelter because of intimate violence and were "clean" and sober for six months. In addition, women were to be assessed for whether they were "ready to make a permanent break from the battering situation," for their ability to follow a service plan, and for the severity of their trauma (if too severe they should be referred elsewhere).

Over the years, the position of the program and of individual staff people

---

56   Transition House newsletter, June 1994.

seemed to vary in tolerance for women who returned to the battering situation and then came back to the shelter. At one point, policy clearly stated women were welcome no matter how often they had gone back. At another point there was an actual policy that a woman would not be welcome back the third time. Mostly, the message was not so clear, and individual staff members and volunteers took their own stances.

Services for women who resided in the shelter included: individual advocacy and weekly support group; weekly parenting skills group; individual vocational counseling; and housing and legal advocacy. Creating and adhering to rules in the house continued to be an area of struggle. The effort to create consistency and safety in the face of constantly changing populations of residents and volunteers had led to what could be seen as some rigidity by the 1990s, as illustrated in this account from one of the staff during that time, reflecting on the experience of a teenage resident at Transition House:

> She was an 18-year-old who had finished high school and …it had not been easy for her. She had been in an abusive relationship, and her abuser was in school with her. She was still really angry and fragile and struggling with that experience. When she came in, staff told her: "You cannot go out to your usual places or have people come visit you." "Yes, yes, yes." She agreed to that. At some point, she was ready to go to her graduation, where the abuser would also be. The shelter director had to sit down with her and say, "You can't go to the graduation," and it devastated her. I remember her saying, "I *earned* this. I *earned* this. I worked *so hard*." And it is no more or less painful than people saying, "But I need to see my mom," or "I miss my abuser. I'm not going back, but I just *miss* my abuser." That was one of the moments when it re-broke my heart all over again. Because this, for everyone, is fresh. She couldn't go to her prom or her graduation. It was many years ago. I think she left the shelter. She needed that moment of accomplishment. It would have been better for us to create a plan, put lots of resources in and make a plan for her to be safe to go and come back. You can force people to say they will sever all ties but you cannot make them do it.

The in-house program for children continued to be a success. "Coping skills, sharing and non-violent ways of expressing emotions are taught to children, who, because of the violence they have witnessed, are often fearful, angry, hostile or destructive to themselves or others."[57] Success with this program led the staff to create a printed curriculum for others to adopt. Services for children at the shelter included: individual counseling (available daily); play and art therapy (individual and group); weekly field trips; and on-site day care from 9 a.m. to 1 p.m. every day except Sunday, and also Friday, 3 p.m. to 5 p.m.

Clinical analysis or mental health intervention had been firmly resisted from the beginning, partly because of the victim-blaming nature of psychological writing about domestic violence in the 1970s and 1980s. In 1976, "feminist therapy" was an oxymoron. By the 1990s there were feminist health collectives with approaches to healing informed by the changes of the 1970s. Feminist therapists, notably Judith Herman, a feminist psychiatrist based in Cambridge,[58] were writing about women victims of violence without victim blaming or pathologizing. At the same time, more women with serious mental health issues were among those staying at the shelter, creating situations staff did not know how to handle. Examples I was given included: What should we do when a teenager is cutting herself and threatening to kill herself? Or when a guest who sometimes experiences herself as a child wants to play in the children's room? As one staff person noted: "People are getting really messed up by being abused." In that context, in spite of the early principles, the staff members finally decided they needed a mental health consultant.

In 1992 a social worker became a volunteer, devoting half a day once or twice a week to Transition House for the next six or seven years. She met regularly as a consultant to the staff, supervised social work interns in the children's room, met with groups of women and sometimes groups of children. Nonetheless, the only formalized qualifications for a paid job at T House remained: embracing diversity and *not* having a mental health degree.

Training, a consistent strength of Transition House, was back up to 32 hours for volunteers, from a lower number in 1982, and in the early 1990s there were about 100 volunteers. Each shift was covered by about four or five volunteers. In addition, volunteers participated in monthly volunteer "round tables" with the volunteer coordinator. Staff had continuing training. This included regular meetings with the Visions consulting group every other month, mostly around multicultural and diversity issues, as well as weekly meetings for "case review" and monthly "clinical supervision" (terms that would have

---

57   Undated and untitled document from Transition House, probably 1995.

58   Herman, J. (1992). *Trauma and Recovery: The Aftermath of Violence from Domestic Abuse to Political Terror.* NY: Basic Books.

been anathema two decades earlier).

Community education was supported by a federal grant. Staff provided training to Cambridge health centers, the Cambridge Women's Commission and DSS. With Emerge, staff met with the police department, with homeless shelters, church groups, and Haitian community groups. T House also collaborated with the Cambridge Substance Abuse Task Force, the State Department of Transitional Assistance, Cambridge-Somerville Legal Services (CASLS), and with Cambridge Hospital for evaluations of children with psychiatric needs.[59]

Transition House continued to operate its 24/7 hotline, answered by both staff and volunteers in shifts. At some point, perhaps when beeper technology created the temptation, an answering service covered some of the evening hours and then relayed the calls to a staff person carrying the beeper. As with all hotlines, there were repeat callers. Some were women in abusive situations who needed to talk and were not ready to leave; week after week they had what seemed to be the same conversation. Others were callers who just needed to talk with someone. One asked (for weeks) where she could buy bug spray. One staff person observed that the volunteers seemed to be capable of endless compassion, even with repeat and ineligible callers.

Staff morale was still high in the early 1990s. One member said, "I loved working with that staff. They were funny, dedicated, had a lot of fun together. So much fun ... There were [also] a lot of fights, a lot of struggle among staff." Some of the struggles pertained to the business of running the shelter, e.g. how much money people should get paid; who should get health insurance; some about managing the women residents, e.g. whether a particular family should have to leave; some about the relations among staff, e.g. how they treated each other, often with regard to the dynamics of race and class.

In an effort to increase accountability, newer staff members were (again) paired with more senior staff (who could be volunteers) in a peer supervisory setup. That arrangement helped, but it did not solve the accountability problem. The collective seemed incapable of decisive action to discipline or terminate. Expressing her sense of helplessness, one respondent said simply: "What can a collective do when someone is not doing her job or should leave?"

By the 1990s, and increasingly through that decade, the optimism of the early women's movement was gone. Many women felt that "there was no end in sight; the beds were always full. How do we put an end to this? In the beginning they really thought they were going to end it. I don't think we [in the 1990s] believed it." Transition House had been fueled by the ideology of

59   Davern, E. (1997). Report on Transition House for DSS.

the 1970s women's movement. Twenty years later faith in the power of refuge, sisterhood, and a feminist analysis to change the lives of survivors of violence (and eventually the world) was shaken.

Ambivalence about ceding power to a smaller group, evident in the 1988 bylaws, continued. Clarifying the 1988 bylaws, the writers of the early 1990s revision limited the CORE to 10 volunteers selected annually for that function and representing the various committees. At the same time, however, "because Transition House is a collective, decisions are made by consensus and all members are entitled to attend and participate in any meeting of CORE or the standing committees."[60] Committees continued to do most of the work of the house. Committees devoted to the DVIP, outreach, battered lesbians, and personnel issues reflected new areas of work and concerns.

Prevention Programming, The DVIP

In 1991 the DVIP reported delivering the three-session curriculum to 5,000 teens at 21 high schools and youth programs, training more than 750 teachers, administrators, youth counselors, and more than 200 peer leaders. The program's "Can't Be Beat" theatre troupe performed to more than 4,000 teens in seven locations. All DVIP curricular units were copresented with male-female teams to model collaboration and open communication between sexes. The same year the program employed four paid staff and 48 volunteers, of whom 32 were teens.[61] Some of the funding came from the state, through DSS; school contracts generated a smaller fraction. Private foundations provided the largest part. However, by 1992 state funding was absent. Corporate and foundation money accounted for more than half; school contracts, fees and curriculum sales for the rest.[62]

The DVIP underwent a growth spurt during the next few years. School-based support groups at Cambridge's one public high school, Cambridge Rindge and Latin School (CRLS), included a group for "young victims of physical and sexual abuse," one for girls who wanted to talk about relationships, and a third group for teen mothers who had experienced violence in their relationships. All freshmen at CRLS received the three-session basic curriculum. Peer-leader training was given annually to 25-50 students, who then presented workshops to middle school students, provided peer counseling, and helped

---

60   DVIP grant application, 1992.

61   Ms. grant application, 1991.

62   1992 grant application. No other specifications.

to develop educational materials.[63]

In the mid-1990s the state Department of Education funded other school districts to provide the project.[64] The DVIP began the first school-based early intervention groups for young offenders, to which high school or middle school boys who "get in trouble for violence or otherwise inappropriate behavior toward a female student or staff" could be referred by school personnel.[65]

In a highly innovative effort to further comprehensive community responses to youth violence, the DVIP worked with the Massachusetts Criminal Justice Training Council to train police officers and health educators in towns throughout the state. The program began with police chiefs selecting three officers to attend the three-day DVIP training. The officers then reached out to local schools to find interested teachers to train with them. After the officers and teachers completed the training, they were to take a proposal to their local school board outlining the need for this type of program and an implementation plan, including parent informational meetings. In addition to developing trainers, this pilot program was "also about facilitating a pro-active role for police officers with youth and families in the communities [where] they work as well as making teachers more aware of the issues their students face on a daily basis. And it provides both groups with connections to battered women's programs locally." [66]

DVIP exhibited its creative spirit also by preparing a proposal that sought funding for a self-help manual for teenage girls and young women, to be called, *"Expect the Best: A Magazine for Young Women on Relationships and Abuse."* The application notes that teenage girls "express a tremendous amount of confusion about how to interpret their partner's actions and expectations." The book was to be in language that young women "of all racial backgrounds and sexual preferences can relate to," with sections specifically for young gay women. It was anticipated that, as with other DVIP materials, teens would do much of the writing. That year DVIP also sought funding to support a group tentatively named the Young Feminist Sorority to focus on projects related to relationship abuse, sexual assault, and harassment. That group would be recruited from the 140 CRLS girls already part of the Cambridge Young Women's Commission.[67]

---

63   Ibid.

64   Department of Education memorandum, July 18, 1996.

65   Carole Sousa, July 1993, testimony.

66   Carole Sousa, 1993, testimony.

67   1992 grant application.

In 1992 the Massachusetts Governor's Commission on Domestic Violence was formed by executive order. Its mission: to advise the administration on "further measures to prevent and protect victims of domestic violence." Carole Sousa was in the first group of commissioners, a tribute to the importance of the DVIP and Transition House's leadership.

Late 1990s

In 1995 Transition House started a new program to help women prepare for the job market. Beginning with women staying at the shelter, it expanded to provide help to those who had left:

> The program is coordinated by a vocational counselor who works on-site with consumers to identify skills and goals and who provides training and services such as computer skills, resume preparation, time management and counseling for women as they enter the job market for the first time. In addition to on-site services, the program coordinator establishes linkages with community educational and vocational resources so that women may return to school, attend ESL and GED classes, participate in work/study programs and access skills which will lead to financial independence.[68]

Clinical language and practice became more evident at T House as the decade proceeded. By the late 1990s the shelter program included weekly case review and service planning meetings as well as one-on-one counseling with women. The children's program included therapeutic individual and group experiences for children.[69] A clinical seminar series in 1996-1997 posed the following topics:

- A feminist perspective on domestic violence (includes "What is feminist therapy? What is the philosophy behind the "collective process" at T House?)
- Compassion with boundaries
- Sexual abuse issues
- Psychopharmacology and health care issues
- Individual and group therapy for children
- Case management issues
- Closure and termination issues

These topics suggest some of the issues and problems facing the staff:

---

68   Transition House, 1997. Descriptions of Programs.
69   May 22, 1997 memo from Robin Braverman, pp. 1-2.

maintaining an allegiance to feminism and the collective process; managing boundaries with residents, balancing advocacy and empowerment; as well as some issues of the residents, e.g. coping with sexual abuse and mental illness.

Through the 1990s the balance of paid to volunteer staff changed. The staff deemed that "it was easier to [pay people] than to train them." There also seemed to be a changed work ethic in the new generation of volunteers; less committed and conscientious, more invested in building their careers than in being part of a movement. By 1997 there were eight full-time and seven part-time paid positions and 40 volunteers (many fewer than five years earlier). All paid staff had been at the organization for fewer than five years. The diversity of the staff and their language capabilities were strengths and included "a Haitian American, a West Indian, a Latina, four African American and five Caucasian staff."[70]

Relationships, between non-collective members and the collective, between paid staff and the volunteer CORE, were showing signs of serious stress. There was one formal grievance, resulting from conflict between two staff people and a number of appeals to the CORE, functioning as a board, for fairer and more equitable treatment of various staff positions. In contrast to the "tyrannical work ethic" of the early years, some staff were trying to protect their own personal time. In addition, there often were not enough staff people on hand to deal effectively or calmly with the issues that came up in the shelter. Without a clear leadership structure, these issues were difficult to negotiate.

The days of laissez-faire oversight, casual reports and blindfolded site visitors were over. Board minutes from March 1997 state: "DSS will spend an entire day at T-House interviewing staff, walking through the House, looking at the personnel policy, intake forms, management structure, and three to four random case files."[71] DSS had had its own internal domestic violence unit since 1992; one of its members did the 1997 evaluation of Transition House.

The ensuing recommendations included eliminating the answering service hours for the hotline: "Women who call in crisis need to be able to reach assistance through the hotline immediately."[72] In addition, the report stated that the screening process was insufficiently inclusive, and objected to the attempts to screen for level of trauma or ability to follow a service plan; the DSS reviewer saw the process as "subjective and rigid." The report expressed concern about adequate food available for the shelter residents and adequate

---

70   Davern, E. (1997). Report on Transition House for DSS, pp. 3-5.

71   Meeting minutes dated April 7, 1997, Item IV.

72   Davern, E., op cit, p. 10.

transportation assistance. It noted the need for a client grievance policy in writing and given to all clients at intake. It recommended that client feedback, including that gathered at exit interviews, be more formally integrated into program planning. There was concern also that too much written information about women residents was in the log books and case records, because "having written detailed information may not be in the best interest of the clients," e.g. in case of court proceedings. All the recommendations concerned advocating for the rights and the voices of the residents and pushed the organization toward more formal business practices.

Not surprisingly, the report was critical of the administrative structure. While recognizing that the collective philosophy "is fundamental to service delivery within the battered women's movement," the report recommended that Transition House devise a plan for clearer roles and administrative functions to assure accountability for staff, funders, and community providers. It also recommended exploring resources for increased support services to battered women and their children in the community and developing a better working relationship with DSS. The report also praised some of the programs; specifically, the DVIP, children's program, and Education and Employment Readiness Program.

The budget mostly grew, with some dips, during the 1990s, reaching the high $600,000s by 1999. Government contracts increasingly provided the major source of revenues (about 2/3 in 1999). Income from foundations, corporations, and the annual appeal still made a substantial contribution, but the days of being supported by individual donors were clearly over, and by the end of the decade Transition House was running a deficit.

In the 1990s Transition House made repeated, almost continuous, efforts to make the governance more efficient and effective. In 1994 the CORE, which had been 10 volunteers, was modified to ensure the governing subgroup represented both volunteers and staff. The CORE was to be made up of three to five paid staff and five to seven volunteers. Volunteer members were selected annually by "all CORE;" paid staff selected their own representatives. Consensus decision-making was still the goal, but "if need be" the CORE could vote, with a majority of at least 75 percent needed for a vote to pass.[73] In 1995, there was again a move to restructure governance. An organizational chart from that year reveals the increased complexity of T House's structure relative to that of the 1980s. (Figure 6: Organization Charts for 1995 and 1988.)

For the first time, Transition House looked outside its current staff and

---

73   Addendum to bylaws, April and May 1994, p. 7.

ORGANIZATION CHART FOR 1988.

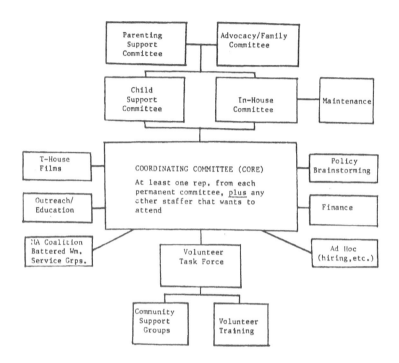

ORGANIZATION CHART FOR 1995.

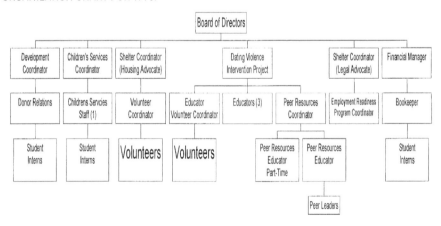

(Figure 6: Organization Charts for 1995 and 1988.)

volunteers for board members—but not very far outside. The board was to be recruited from former volunteers and members of the consulting group that had worked with the staff. Then, in early 1996, "The board agreed that Transition House would benefit by expanding its board eligibility requirements to the larger community. A formal means of communicating from the various programs and committees to the board has yet to be instituted."[74]

In spite of these efforts to "fix" the governance structure, the signs of distress increased. The organization suffered serious financial trouble, and the board decided to cut all employees' salaries, which had been raised the year before, but could not be supported. With impending pay cuts the staff decided to limit The Collective to six of the paid staff. As all collective members were paid equally, excluding some paid staff from The Collective would protect some salaries at the expense of others, while clearly violating the spirit of collective governance. Relations among the staff were strained, with a number of complaints to the board.   One board member reflected: "It was the depths: women fighting women." Three key long-term volunteers/staff resigned in 1996, largely in protest of board decisions relating to staff complaints. Their departures left important roles to be filled and must have further damaged morale.

A retreat, to be facilitated by a paid outsider, was planned for February 1997. Notes from a staff/board meeting in January 1997 convey the frustration people felt. Most often expressed was concern about the governance: "Too many people deciding every issue;" "Without defined accountability at T House, things often fall through the cracks;" "There are not clear guidelines as to who makes decisions and how these decisions should be carried out;" "When people are hired they are usually not told of the managerial duties they have as collective members;" "Everyone has power, yet nobody has power." There was also concern about relations with the community: "We don't have strong contacts in the community;" "T House doesn't have a strong or positive presence in Cambridge." Perhaps the most disturbing concern for many was that possibly "The staff frustration does seep down and sometimes affects the quality of services." There was general agreement that long-term planning was needed and that the "quality of service delivery" was crucial.

Another outside consultant (who had gotten her early training through Transition House) worked with the staff through much of the year to create a vision for the budget process by agreeing on short- and longer-term goals.[75]

74   "Job Description for Transition House's Board," undated. Quote comes from the end.

75   Braverman, R., May 22, 1997 report concerning the Program Vision of the Staff.

Short-term goals reflected the need for more confidential space inside the shelter, stipends for certain volunteers who were supervisors and/or took needed hotline shifts, more outreach efforts, and more reliable basics (maintenance, food supply) in the shelter. Short-term goals for the children's program included more training for staff, additional staffing, refurbishing of space, more after-school hours, and more training of public school teachers. Longer-term goals included transitional housing, more structure, and requirements (including budget training) for residents to increase success after shelter.

The board members worked valiantly to stay on top of difficulties on many fronts. The building needed repairs, some of which appeared to be major. Even with reduced expenses, T House was running a deficit;[76] funding agencies were dissatisfied with aspects of the operation; dissension continued between the board and the staff, with the latter feeling disempowered and demeaned; staff accused the board of racial insensitivity. Describing the situation gently, minutes of the April 1997 meeting note that "everyone had good intentions in their roles, and the organization had serious turf issues that a better organizational structure may solve."

In June, the board decided that a small Executive Committee of the board, to include one staff person, would meet "frequently and regularly" to deal with crucial items. These items included: hiring a management consultant and recruiting new board members with legal and management skills. In addition to all the other pressing business, the board had to deal with the staff grievances.

By the fall of 1997, the board reached a consensus that it "would begin the process of hiring a part-time executive director [ED]."[77] As the process for hiring an ED began, the board also amended the bylaws, transferring to the new ED the responsibilities formerly held by the management group/collective/paid staff, giving the board the authority to assume the ED's duties in an emergency, defining quorum and majorities for board votes. The days of consensus decision-making would be over: "a simple majority of the quorum affirms the vote." The board also amended personnel policies to give the ED supervisory responsibility.[78]

The first person designated to be Transition House's ED was hired in December 1997 and resigned in late January, 1998. At that point the board looked for outside consultation. A memo from the board states: "Currently, Transition House is looking to change from a collective form of governance

---

76   Board minutes, November 3, 1997.

77   Memo to the board from Mary Thornton, October 5, 1997.

78   Proposal for Changes to Bylaws, memo to board of directors, December 1, 1997.

to an Executive Director and a more hierarchical organizational structure. At the same time, we have had the financial manager leave the agency. We hope to reorganize and combine positions to better manage the agency. In the interim, however, we need the skills of both an administrator and a finance director."[79]

New board members were selected early in 1998, and they went to work seeking resumes of candidates for the ED position. Meanwhile, the board needed to attend to issues related to fire safety, pressing financial concerns (a bare-bones budget of $587,289 for 1998 still exceeded revenue by about $14,000), and a succession of staff grievances, one of which culminated in a lawsuit. These issues affirmed the urgent need to clarify and update personnel policies.

Yves-Rose SaintDic, consistently considered the first ED of Transition House, was hired in May 1998. Yves-Rose had volunteered at T House, and her sister had for many years been the bookkeeper. She came, therefore, with a deep knowledge of the organization, and both staff and board members already knew her. As a Haitian-American she brought a valued connection to a local population Transition House was eager to serve better.

Conclusion

Through the 1990s, Transition House continued to be a safe refuge for women fleeing abuse. Its programs were in many ways responsive to the needs of the women and children who stayed there and the realities of the environment in which they hoped to become economically viable and housed. To meet those needs Transition House developed and maintained programs on parenting skills, educational and employment readiness, individual vocational counseling, housing and legal advocacy, various therapies (individual, play, art) for children, and on-site day care for children. It was also exploring non-emergency housing options.

The hotline continued to be an effective resource for women struggling with abuse. The DVIP continued to spread its message, materials, and influence. It ran quite independently of the shelter, although its leader was active in running Transition House until she left in the mid-1990s. The children's program continued to be in the forefront of responding to the needs of children exposed to violence in the home.

The foundational positions against hierarchical organization and against including a mental health framework in the understanding of battered women gradually eroded through the 1990s. From the beginning, the assumption had

---

79   Bridger, Francis. Letter to Management Consulting Services, February 9, 1998.

been that a movement organization could not be a social service organization. T House was created as the former, and was becoming the latter, in spite of many who resisted.

The gradual shift toward a service organization was often attributed to the pressures of funders,[80] which were real. One T House employee, who had worked previously in another domestic violence shelter, said, "success led to the loss of autonomy, integrity. This cancer has eaten every single movement. Once you are in a state of economic dependency, they change how you view the problems."

Yet, there were also other forces in play. Increasingly, self-help and peer support were not sufficient to equip most of the residents of the house to work and live on their own. More of the women came from immigrant cultures (the hotline information sheet from the 1990s has check boxes for nine languages and room for more), and the early effort to screen out women with mental illness and drug addiction had failed. At least as important, the social, economic and political environment had changed. Affordable housing was harder to find; welfare was being "reformed" in a way that made it less available; jobs for which the women were prepared were increasingly scarce. In addition, the women's movement out of which the shelter had grown was no longer a dominant force sustaining a political analysis. The analysis of domestic violence in terms only of male oppression of women seemed insufficiently complex; the belief that women's empowerment would reform structured inequities relating to gender, race, and class seemed illusory. At the same time, the staff (and what was now called the domestic violence, as opposed to battered women's, field) was becoming more aware of the psychological and cultural complexities of leaving abusive relationships and the costs of criminal justice interventions. As the original political analysis was losing its power, the ascendance in the culture of "trauma" as a concept pulled those working with battered women and their children toward a mental health framework. It was difficult to maintain the empowering experiences of self-help and mutual help in this context.

Transition House was able to sustain and grow its programs, but struggled constantly with its governing structure. Running the shelter as a collective had been difficult, really from the beginning. To the dedicated people who maintained this form of governance for decades, the power of their engagement in the processes it demanded was worth the costs in efficiency and clarity of role. The collective process was where consciousness-raising, movement-building, and running the shelter came together; and T House identified with all

---

80 See, for instance, Schechter, S. (1982), op cit, p. 95.

those purposes and with that process. Letting go of the collective may have signified letting go of its movement identity. To say it was not easy to let go of the collective understates that loss. Organizational problems really forced the decision, but still it was hard. Ultimately, in 1996, the collective ended with the development of a real board of directors. From 1996 to 1998 the new board, composed primarily of long-time volunteers, worked tirelessly to keep the organization viable in spite of daunting challenges.

Ending her term in September 1998, the board president wrote about her own doubts about terminating the collective; but she finished with: "Step back and see what we have done: we have saved this organization from fiscal ruin, taken steps to make it a place where people can live and work with dignity again, and most importantly, we have kept the doors to T-House open to the women whose lives depend on it. This is not a small, careless thing. This is good work."[81]

Transition House had been a collective for more than 20 years, much longer than most other feminist organizations that began in the 1970s, maybe longer than any other running a shelter. In 1998 the first ED was hired, and a new chapter began.

---

81   Simenas, N. Letter dated September 13, 1998.

CHAPTER 4
1998 to 2004: Reorganizing for a New Era

The external challenges of the 1990s increased in the early 2000s and became even more dramatic in the later part of the decade. In the context of these challenges, the first two EDs (1998 to 2001; 2001 to 2004), in very different ways, oversaw hopeful changes in the shelter building itself, the functioning of the staff, and the relationship of Transition House with the city of Cambridge as well as new programs.

The First Executive Director, 1998 to 2001

After very gradual and ambivalent shifts in basic assumptions during the earlier 1990s, the fundamental organization of Transition House changed, and the last two years of the decade were filled with action based on new assumptions. It seemed a new start of a differently structured organization; one that maintained its original purpose of sheltering and empowering battered women, but with less confidence about its goal of ending domestic violence. It had new programs, new vision, energy and hopes; but not its original commitments to peer help, consciousness-raising, and movement building. According to one staff person: "It was a culture of respect, but not feminist." Although opposed to the changes herself, one board member wrote: "Transition House is a hierarchy now. The Collective is only a memory and we are very lucky to have Yves-Rose ... as our director ...We still employ a feminist perspective, but now it's more refined, more socially acceptable ... and definitely quieter."[82]

Yves-Rose SaintDic came with a clear sense of her priorities as ED. As she told me, these were: create a more effectively functioning staff ("It was a highly dysfunctional group when I got hired"); improve links to immigrant communities; improve relationship with the City of Cambridge; raise money

---

82   Doughty, W. Transition House newsletter, Fall 1999.

to fix the building. Yves-Rose served as ED until August of 2001.

Yves-Rose and the board gave immediate attention to personnel policies, safety issues in the shelter, and fund-raising. By August a 40-hour week was implemented for all full-time staff, and there was 24-hour coverage of the shelter.[83] In addition, a number of fund-raising events were planned. The rest of 1998 saw efforts to make new connections to the Cambridge Women's Commission and Cambridge Hospital, to reach out to "prominent people in Cambridge and elsewhere to get support for T House, to exert influence in the legislative area,"[84] and to begin a long-range planning process. When she got there, Yves-Rose said, "Everyone was doing everything, from raising money to fixing plumbing, and you can't focus on the bigger issues." Prior to long-range planning, she proposed some structural changes in staffing to clarify the roles and accountability and also proposed hiring an outside consultant, possibly a social worker, to meet with the staff. She also brought people onto the board who had not been volunteers.

In November, the board held a strategic-planning retreat, identifying strengths and weaknesses of Transition House, summarized in reports on the internal and external environments. Board members began work on a strategic plan in early 1999. Internally, the report indicates that the house, itself, was a major asset, but it "is dilapidated and in need of serious repair." It notes that the Cambridge location is a strength, but "our lack of connection to the community is a glaring weakness." Financially, it continues, the situation was better than it had been for many years, but the leadership needed more unrestricted funds. In addition, the report identifies a new mission statement as a priority, the old one seen as "outdated and unclear." With respect to the organizational culture, it notes that, "our weaknesses presently overwhelm our strengths …"[85] Low morale, lack of cultural understanding, disrespect, an overworked and burned-out staff, and the need for more training and more consistently professional behavior were mentioned. The hiring of Yves-Rose was seen as a "hugely positive step," as were the retreat and strategic- planning process.

The closing paragraph of The Internal Environment section of the strategic-planning report of early 1999 (reproduced below) reveals the distance travelled from the ethos of the early days when peer help was the program; empowerment, the goal; and "client" not an acceptable term for women seeking refuge at Transition House. The board explained:

---

83   Board minutes, August 3, 1998.

84   Board minutes, October 5, 1998.

85   Transition House: The Internal Environment, pp.1-2 from 1999 strategic planning report.

Our programs haven't changed enough with the times, however. Questions remain about whether we are focused enough on who our clients are, and whether we have a firm and structured enough program. A lack of staffing is considered a real problem, impacting our ability to provide more services to the women and children in the house. Our mental health services are also weak, an area that is an increasingly important part of the work we do. In terms of program recordkeeping and statistics, we are weak. There is not agreement on what outcomes we want to be measuring, and we rely too heavy [sic] on anecdotal evidence. Our exit interview process is not working, and we have almost no long-term follow-up once a woman and her family leave the shelter. Finally, it is felt that too many women go to another shelter following their time at T-house, and too many end up returning to their batterer.[86]

In the external environment report, the board summarized federal, state, and city priorities, initiatives, and changes. It then considered how those aligned with the areas identified in the strategic plan. T House was financially dependent on the government (on all levels) and its agents.

Yves-Rose hired a new shelter director who had many years of experience working in another domestic violence shelter and was the first T House full-time employee with training as a therapist. Among her first initiatives, the new shelter director started an intern program, with students from local schools doing individual and group therapy with the residents. She saw this as a way for the women residents to process the effects of trauma on their lives and for the students to understand trauma from a political perspective. With her background in shelter work and her therapeutic training she held a double perspective that fit the times. Volunteers staffed the hotline and worked with the women to keep the house in order; paid staff did advocacy, overnights, and the children's program. Reflecting on these years, the shelter director said, "The staff was strong; morale was fine … " What was not fine, in her view, was the condition of the building: "The physical space was shabby, not an inviting place to come and heal. It was an old house in bad shape … a very depressing building. The office I had—if I met with someone I had to close the door with a towel, because the door wouldn't close." The annual budget for 1998 was a little more than $633,000, all of which was needed to run the programs.

Yves-Rose hired Mary Gilfus, a faculty member from a local school of

---

86   Transition House: The Internal Environment. Op cit, p. 3.

social work, as a consultant to the staff. Mary held a series of meetings with Yves-Rose and led four intensive workshops with the staff. The goal was "to review and revitalize the shelter programs and policies."[87] One of the products of this consultation was a new Welcome Book for residents to replace the manual. It included clear statements of the rules for residents, as well as the rules' intent to support a safe and secure environment. It outlined processes for dealing with infractions and included an attached residents' Bill of Rights.

The consultant's 1999 report identifies key issues confronting the shelter, including:

- changing external demands (e.g. more competitive funding environment and increased demands for documentation and evaluation);
- changing population needs (e.g. women with more complex social, economic and cultural issues and increasing lack of available post-shelter housing); and
- changing internal structure of T House.

She noted that "original values, visions, goals and traditions are up for question," and asked the staff to consider (among other questions): "What does empowerment of battered women mean in the age of 'managed care'? Can we support women's full power to make their own choices or are we required to force them to reach pre-determined goals and outcomes? Is there a balance? What is a 'successful outcome' for a maximum 90-day shelter stay... ?"[88]

Mary's report states, "We came out of the process with a 'road map' that all agreed to work on ... "[89] Staff would take more responsibility for ensuring that all programs take place as scheduled; the director would develop a plan to provide all staff with increased administrative and clinical supervision and to provide in-service training; individual "recovery plans" for each resident would be regularly reviewed; rules and criteria for being asked to leave would be clarified; the program would begin to develop new evaluation tools and plans. The report notes: "One of the many apparent strengths of this program is that it is a diverse multicultural (and increasingly international) organization able to provide shelter services to very diverse populations. These are the kinds of strengths that the organization should celebrate and build upon." In her interview with me Mary noted that the staff were "underpaid and overworked. There was not enough staff for basic functions."

---

87   Gilfus, M. (1999). Report to Transition House board, p. 1.

88   Gilfus, M. (1999). Op cit, p. 2.

89   Ibid.

Transition House initiated many new programs and strengthened community relationships in 1999. For example:

- Refugee and Immigration Services funds supported work with the local Haitian population at the shelter and also with allied agencies in Somerville and Mattapan.[90]
- An AmeriCorps grant funded 10 volunteers to serve for a year at T House.
- An after-school program for young batterers in Cambridge continued, and a 24-hour hotline specifically for teen callers, "Teen Respect," began.[91]
- The ED and board president met with the board of RESPOND, Somerville's domestic violence agency, to explore ways for the two organizations to work together.

Some changes reflected the increasing turn toward professionally trained staff, notably:

- A second clinical consultant was hired to work with the DVIP staff and, when needed, one-on-one with women in the shelter.
- Within the shelter a children's service position was filled by someone with a Master's degree in social work.

In addition:

- Mandatory volunteer "round tables" were held every six weeks at which volunteers could discuss issues arising in their work, be informed of new volunteer opportunities at T House, and catch up on other T House developments.
- Search began for a development director in anticipation of a capital campaign to fund shelter renovations, with a goal of $800,000 to come from the state, the city, and private donors.
- Meetings were held with an architect about renovation of the house.
- The 25th anniversary event was planned.

By the end of the 1990s, it had become impossible for most women to find housing within a 90-day stay, and Transition House saw the need to provide non-emergency housing (transitional housing) options, for which federal funds through the Department of Housing and Urban Development (HUD)

---

90   Board minutes, March 1, and April 5, 1999.

91   Board minutes, February 1999.

could be sought. Cambridge had a Homeless Services Planning Commission, in which T House became a participant in 1998, as it began the process of planning for its own Transitional Living Program.

Meanwhile, the day-to-day work of the shelter continued. The monthly report for Direct Services (shelter) in July, 1999 details that Transition House:

- Served 10 women and eight children.
- Offered two ongoing support groups, attendance at 80 percent.
- Took two women to court to get restraining orders extended.
- Brought residents to an ex-volunteer's house for a day of swimming and relaxing.
- Coordinated another beauty day for haircutting and manicures at Diane's Salon.
- Had two residents accepted into Transitional Living Programs.
- Had two residents accepted to rent a house in a suburb of Boston.
- Received a call from an ex-resident to let us know she had her baby.
- Established a new system for keeping better track of ex-resident files.
- Offered our first clinical in-service training. It went great!
- Arranged for food allotment to be picked up from Massachusetts Emergency Food Assistance Program.
- Updated the Web page.

Reflecting on her experience, Yves-Rose said, "We may be pulling our hair out; how are we going to pay people? But you go upstairs or go to the children's room, they tell you you're saving their lives. That's what made it work." And, she added: "The board was amazing." In spite of the struggle with finances, governance, and building maintenance, the women and children staying at T House were the priority. One long-term volunteer, CORE member, and board chair who worked tirelessly through the administrative turmoil of the 1990s, looking back, acknowledged, "It felt like a safe place for everyone. It still feels that way."

The year 2000 began with a stabilized staff, a functioning new structure, new board members, new programs in the community, a strategic plan, a capital campaign, the impending move to a temporary location during rehabilitation of the shelter, and planning for a 25th anniversary celebration. In addition, there were continuing issues demanding work: revising the Transition House bylaws to reflect the new governance structure and expanded programs; continued attention to an unsettled lawsuit from the late 1990s; and an anticipated need to apply for new funding from DSS as a current contract expired.[92]

The board, with new membership alongside some of the veterans, was working to formalize Transition House's processes; to clearly define all staff, board, and committee positions and duties; and to hold people accountable for complying with laws, regulations, funder agreements, policies, and general professional behavior norms.

The board retreat in 2000 worked to "develop a new vision" for the organization and establish new strategic goals. Discussion in that meeting included whether Transition House should be "women-centered" or "community-centered." Different understandings of "women-centered," particularly between African-American and white women, were addressed, with acknowledgment that, "the empowerment of women is linked to working with men."[93] The mission statement was revised to read: "Transition House is committed to the prevention and cessation of domestic violence through services which provide safety for women and children and empower women to thrive."[94]

The capital campaign was ambitious: rehabilitate and expand the existing shelter, increasing capacity from seven to 11 bedrooms; keep the shelter open at a different site during reconstruction; establish a greater community presence with administrative offices separate from the shelter; operate a dual-diagnosis (sic) domestic violence and substance abuse transitional living program; purchase a second site in Cambridge for that new program. Each goal had specific objectives and a timetable.[95] As it turned out, the financial goal of $800,000 was met; the shelter building was completely rehabilitated; and the administrative offices moved (temporarily) off-site. The purchase of a second site did not happen, and a transitional housing program was ultimately delayed until 2002.

In August 2000 the shelter moved to a house a few miles away in Chelsea. The administrative offices moved into rented space in Cambridge. Construction began in October 2000, and residents and staff moved into the rehabilitated shelter building in the summer of 2001. A staff member hired just before the renovation recalled, "The transformation was unbelievable." The formerly depressing and crowded building felt bright and welcoming. Administrative offices returned to the shelter building until April 2002, when the second ED moved them (again) into their own space.[96]

---

92 Board minutes, January 2000.

93 Notes from board retreat, May 6, 2000.

94 Ibid.

95 Report of June 6, 2000.

96 Transition House six-month evaluation of ED, March 2002.

While the shelter was being renovated, Transition House celebrated its 25th anniversary at the Museum of Science in Boston on February 15, 2001. As part of the evening's festivities the board chairperson recognized the Transition House founders, and a special award was given to Katherine Triantafillou, recognizing both her role as legal adviser in the early years and in initiating Cambridge's citywide Domestic Violence Free Zone campaign while she was a city councilor. The evening was deemed a "great event" and cleared $2,000 to $3,000.

Changes in the children's program illustrate the efforts to coordinate with allied agencies and groups. The program worked with the new Child Witness to Violence program at the Cambridge Guidance Center and met with an outside organization (Horizons Initiative), which provided volunteers to homeless shelters, to explore their coordinating the volunteers in the Transition House children's program.

The staff positions in January 2001 (the last three unfilled at the time) were:

- Executive Director
- Development Officer
- Shelter Director
- Consultant/Trainer (with a Master's degree in social work)
- Haitian Project: 24-hour facilitator and male co-leader
- Office Manager/Bookkeeper
- Volunteer Coordinator: 30 hours
- DVIP Male Facilitator
- DVIP Female Facilitator
- Case Manager
- House Manager: 7 a.m. to 3 p.m.
- House Manager: 3 p.m. to 11 p.m.
- Overnight Sleep Staff
- Weekend Staff
- Relief Staff
- Children Coordinator
- Community Program Coordinator
- Employment and Education Readiness Coordinator

With the organizational changes, staff performance had become more reliable, and morale seemed good. Yves-Rose managed to hold the staff more accountable without creating or encountering tremendous resistance, in spite of an environment in which many long-term volunteers were mourning the loss of the collective. A staff member adds: "[She] did a good job making people feel comfortable moving forward."

Volunteers answered the hotline, took shifts in the shelter, and interacted with the women. As had consistently been the case, people were profoundly affected by the experience of being trained by and volunteering at Transition House. A volunteer who began in the late 1990s and continued as an employee, captured some of the feeling of many volunteers: "I learned a tremendous amount and met amazing people. It shaped a lot of who I am today. In small agencies with a tremendous amount of work and too few people, there are opportunities." At the same time, she admitted, "it was challenging to manage the sense of overwhelm, keep up energy and hope … There was never quite enough of what people needed and deserved."

The Haitian program was, by its nature, a community program, working with allied agencies in Cambridge and nearby towns. The DVIP managed the Teen Respect hotline, contracted with schools in a number of neighboring towns, and was updating its curriculum. Transition House participated in a number of state and local meetings, including the Cambridge Domestic Violence Task Force, the Governor's Commission on Domestic Violence, the Same Sex Domestic Violence Roundtable, the Middlesex County DA's Domestic Violence Breakfast Forum, and The Coalition, which, during the 1990s, became Jane Doe, Inc.

Organization representatives had also become active partners in Cambridge's Homeless Services Planning meeting, and in September 2000 Transition House submitted proposals for a Transitional Living Program for domestic violence survivors with substance abuse issues. Many possible locations were considered, including the present building which would mean finding a new home for the emergency shelter. The grant received was less than half of what was needed, and a collaborative program was sought. That plan was for the YWCA-Cambridge to provide five rooms for the program.[97]

Yves-Rose announced in April 2001 that she would resign that August. As the first ED, she had managed considerable change. There was a newly structured staff, new employees, and new members of the board. Roles had been formalized, accountability increased, and morale improved. The staff included two people working with the immigrant community; the capital campaign and house rehabilitation were successful; the 25th anniversary celebration in collaboration with Cambridge was testimony to an improved relationship with the city.

Yet, it was an exhausting job. It was frustrating to realize continually that

---

97   Board minutes, February 2001.

90 days was not enough time for the women who stayed at the shelter. There were tensions with some board members and volunteers. Some of the volunteers had been there for more than 10 or even 20 years. They were dedicated, knowledgeable, and consistent; and they were used to being their own bosses. In addition, Yves-Rose felt too much fell to the ED, and it was hard to stay focused on the big picture. Nonetheless, she added: "You couldn't pay me enough, but it almost didn't matter, seeing the women's lives transformed." When she resigned, the board realized "what a big hole was left" without her. Her resignation also coincided with a national recession in 2001, which led to drastic cuts from some of T House's major funders.

With Yves-Rose's resignation, the board had "a lengthy discussion [about] what has contributed to the current situation and about reorganizing the agency."[98] "The current situation" that concerned them included a shortage of funds, exacerbated by the funding cuts, and a sense that the organization needed more administrative personnel, that too much had depended on the ED.[99] Some board members felt as though Yves-Rose seemed irreplaceable partly because she had done so much without their involvement. Others felt that difficulties were inevitable in the transition from a crisis period in the late 1990s to the stability and patterns that were now established. In any case, there was, again, talk of reorganizing: "The board needs to examine the issue of the self-empowerment model."[100] They decided to increase the administrative staff by hiring an external affairs/fund-raising person as well as a new ED. In the search for a new ED, Transition House abandoned its history of a compressed pay scale between the lowest and highest paid staff, realizing that the ED salary needed to meet the "industry standard" to attract good enough candidates.[101] The term "industry standard" in the board minutes is another signifier of how much had changed since the 1970s.

Beyond Shelter, Expanding Housing Programs

Reflecting the board's focus on strengthening the administrative side, the ED position was offered to Elsbeth Kalendarian in July 2001, to start in September. Trained as a dentist and experienced as a health care administrator, she possessed some of the administrative skills the board felt Transition House needed, although she lacked experience with the issue of domestic violence

---

98   Board minutes, March 2001.

99   Ibid.

100   Board minutes, April 2001.

101   Board minutes, July 2001.

or with social justice organizations.

Elsbeth moved the organizational processes further toward hierarchy and accountability. As she said herself: "I made it much more hierarchical; or the board did by hiring me." She instituted regular performance evaluations for staff and volunteers and aimed to get better statistics on how the various programs were working. "We had very good statistics from the DVIP; for other programs we needed to have some numbers," she said. She recalls wanting "to make the vision bigger, beyond shelter for 11 women, to get more resources."

She rebuilt the board, enlarging its membership from 12 to 16, and adding more professionals, including some men. As one board member said, "it was no longer movement people." The shelter director at the time saw the board becoming "an upper class white professional board [with] more men, and powerful men without a social justice perspective." Elsbeth also envisioned a much larger advisory board. The administrative offices moved out of the shelter, which she felt was important to protect the administrators from being pulled into the minutiae of each day at the shelter. For the first time, the board and the ED were not in immediate and constant contact with the operations of the shelter, which some volunteers and staff perceived as a loss. One employee reported: "I saw the organization going away from community, history, the feminist movement. It was a critical time for Transition House."

At the 2002 board retreat, the members partly devoted their attention to the vision of the organization. By then, the board included professionals with advanced degrees in medicine and psychology. The board wrestled with discrepancies between "the empowerment model" and "clinical models." They grappled with questions, such as, "How can we empower women who have severe clinical issues? When does the safety/well-being of children override the empowerment model?" The organization's struggles with its central values are reflected in the frequent rewordings of the mission statement, which seem to reflect a tension between a new emphasis on "viable, effective, relevant interventions," and a continuing emphasis on a "diverse and culturally sensitive setting" and "empowerment." After multiple changes, the mission statement in the Spring 2003 newsletter read:

> The Mission of Transition House is to prevent and stop domestic violence through education and intervention. Our purpose is to provide the refuge and support services, education and empowerment skills that will enable battered women to access permanent safety and well-being for themselves and their children. We strive to dispel the notion that domestic violence is inevitable, to provide violence

prevention education to children and adults; to educate the community about the realities of domestic and dating violence, and to offer viable, effective relevant intervention strategies to other providers of services to battered women and their children.[102]

The board continued to formalize its organizational structure, as well as the staff's.

By the early 2000s Transition House was receiving funds from many different state, federal, and city programs. About one-third of total revenue came from DSS, including some federal money passed through DSS. Funding also came from the Massachusetts Department of Public Health (MDPH); US Health and Human Services (HHS) through New England Medical Center; US Department of Justice under the Victims of Crime Act (VOCA) and Violence Against Women Act (VAWA); Massachusetts Department of Education (DOE); and US Housing and Urban Development (HUD) through Cambridge Community Development Block grants. Altogether, government grants accounted for about 75 percent of the budget. United Way contributed about 10 percent; private foundations and individuals made up the rest.

As a result of so many funders, bookkeeping and accounting had become complicated and challenging. With turnover in the bookkeeping position, a number of administrative office moves, and a change in the ED, the bookkeeping had "fallen behind," and various administrative and record-keeping functions were not in compliance with accepted practices, as the 2001 audit made clear.

Elsbeth worked to rectify these lapses and improve the financial systems. As the board's mid-year 2002 review of the ED states: "the budget was not a meaningful management tool for a significant period of time prior to Elsbeth's arrival at Transition House." Subsequent audits revealed significant accounting errors related to the rehabilitation of the building, which left Transition House with a substantial reduction in net assets.[103]

Efforts to increase private fund-raising in 2002 and 2003 were less successful than hoped, and a number of government contracts were reduced or eliminated in those years, leaving the agency unable to make up completely the earlier losses. To balance the budget some cost-cutting measures, including staff reductions, were made. With the help of increased income from contracts, subsequent budgets for FY 2004 and 2005 balanced.

---

102   Transition House newsletter, Spring 2003, back page.

103   Finance opinion memo, April 5, 2005, in merger binder.

The renovated shelter was designed to serve 11 families. However, there was funding for only eight of the rooms; as a result, the remaining three rooms were unused until 2003. Transition House attempted to raise the money through an "adopt a room" campaign, but it fell short. At the same time, RESPOND, the domestic violence organization in Somerville, needed shelter space while its own shelter was rebuilt. The decision was made to rent four rooms, three for women residents and children, to RESPOND.

For the staff, the years between 2003 and 2005, during which the organization shared its shelter space with RESPOND, were taxing ones. The arrangement obviously served an important financial purpose for Transition House and a pressing need for RESPOND. At the same time, it was somewhat confusing to the T House staff (and probably also to the RESPOND staff). As the (then) shelter director mused in her interview, "Are they tenants or colleagues? They had an ED, too ... The relationship was difficult." In many ways the two organizations had similar missions and services, but their organizational cultures were not well matched.

While Transition House staff members struggled to work with the RESPOND staff, they were dealing also with other stressors. There had been staff reductions to deal with the budget shortfall at the same time that new space was rented for the administrative staff. The shelter's frontline staff felt vulnerable, under-resourced, and somewhat resentful of money going away from the shelter to fund the other office. These strains were exacerbated by what felt like an absence of administrative support, especially during the period when the shelter space was shared with RESPOND. When Elsbeth began as ED, she focused on board issues, "fiscal rigor," and on finding ways to grow the organization. Her interactions with the staff were mostly in monthly meetings, and she instituted regular performance evaluations. One board member noted: "We were excellent at finding ways to help and empower residents. [We were] weak with doing that for staff."

Some of the staff and volunteers, particularly those who remembered the collective, were angry about the direction in which Elsbeth was moving the organization. One member of the management team, who had been hired by Yves-Rose said, "It felt like two sides at war. Elsbeth ignored the history. She tried to create an organization without learning about its past. It felt disrespectful to the past." There was also some concern that the staff was stratifying along racial lines, with people of color at the low end of the pay scale. Elsbeth noted this concern during her first year and supported a diversity task force, staff training, and outside consultation to the board and staff.[104]

Volunteers still acquired intensive training in three 32-hour sessions, now done collaboratively with other domestic violence agencies. Fifty to 100 volunteers were trained each year for all the participating domestic violence programs. Volunteers at T House felt considerable solidarity with direct service staff in the shelter. In both groups, many felt alienated by the change from open boundaries among board, staff, and volunteers, to the current more distant administration in its own office and more professional board.

Volunteer roles had also been somewhat formalized, with limitations placed on the degree of personal involvement or friendship that volunteers could have with residents. The volunteer roundtable notes of March 18, 2002 suggest that volunteers should not exchange phone numbers or addresses with residents. The notes explain, "The nature of the relationship mandates that the volunteer act as a peer support, which is different than a friend. The nature of the relationship is not that of two individuals giving equally of themselves." With the increased formalization of volunteer roles, some volunteers felt ineffective. One reported: "I mostly did clerical work or baby-sitting."

Transition House gradually became less dependent on volunteers for direct service work and day-to-day operations during this decade. Many factors impacted this change. With the move to Chelsea, some volunteers had dropped out either because of the commute or because the temporary facility was just too small to handle extra people. With changes in the larger culture, including white women's increased participation in paid work, volunteering was reduced nationally between 1974 and 1989.[105] As Transition House adopted more clinical perspectives, graduate-level social work interns gradually replaced some of the volunteer roles.

Community outreach activities had greatly expanded, and relations with Cambridge became more open and active. The shelter's secret location and long-held principle that visitors had first to go through training before entering the shelter had contributed to the perception of its "bunker mentality." The administrative office's new location in rented space apart from the shelter helped to change that. The focus on housing programs beyond the emergency shelter also brought Transition House closer to the city and to those concerned about the homeless population.

The DVIP, Transition House's long-time ambassador to the city, continued,

---

104   Fall 2002 ED self-evaluation.

105   Corporation for National and Community Service (2006). *Volunteer growth in America: trends since 1974*. p. 2. Retrieved from www.nationalservice.gov. September, 2017.

but struggled with cuts in funding in 2003. With creative partnering DVIP maintained their activity in schools, joining with City Year in 2003-2004 and with Boston College School of Social Work in 2004-2005 to recruit part- and full-time volunteers.

During her tenure (September 2001 to May 2004), Elsbeth focused on new housing programs, with the Transitional Living Program (TLP) as a high priority. She imagined a continuum of housing and services from shelter to more permanent housing, modeled on the health care system's flow from inpatient to rehab to outpatient treatments, with which she was familiar. She was certainly not alone in recognizing the need for housing options after shelter. Planning had begun in prior years, and there was broad agreement that three months in an emergency shelter, by its nature somewhat chaotic, was not sufficient for most women to find stable permanent housing under the present economic realities. Nor was the shelter stay enough for many of the residents to gain the skills and support needed to become economically viable.

Ronit Barkai was hired in 2002 to develop and manage the new longer-term housing programs. She had most recently worked at another domestic violence organization. About a year later, the TLP outgrew its space at the YWCA-Cambridge and an effort began to find a new permanent site. Many possible locations were investigated for purchase, but a permanent new building was not found, and there was some pressure to move quickly in order to retain HUD funding. In 2003 the TLP relocated to four scattered-site apartments. The TLP provided nine to 24 months of supported housing, funded largely by HUD and Cambridge Housing Authority (CHA) grants. Because of the federal funding, it had the limitation that undocumented immigrants cannot qualify. Around the same time, Transition House contracted to provide services to a 40-unit supported-living complex in Somerville, the Kent Street Apartments. Kent Street tenants were all low income, some disabled. Although there was no direct connection to the Transition House domestic violence mission, the board reasoned that providing residential services was useful experience as the agency moved toward more residential programs of its own. It also brought in money. In December 2003, T House opened a Permanent Supported Housing Program, which provides long-term housing in scattered-site apartments for women and families with a history of domestic violence who are homeless and disabled.

By the time Elsbeth left, the TLP housed four single women and three families; there were six units of Permanent Supported Housing, as well as support for the 40 units at Kent Street, the last not specifically for survivors of domestic violence. The next year (2005), the TLP offered five units at two different sites, housing four single women and five small families. Program services included monthly training on varied topics (self-defense, career counseling, e.g.), educational and employment readiness, and technical and financial assistance. Residents were required to save 20 percent of their income toward their move to more permanent housing. Program fees were 10 percent of the woman's income.

Elsbeth announced her resignation in the Spring of 2004. Although she recalls having given appropriate notice, staff and board members from that time report being taken by surprise. Without time for a well-planned transition, there was an immediate need for interim leadership. Once again, the resignation of the ED ushered in a period of self-questioning for the board.

CHAPTER 5
2004 to 2008: Leadership and Identity Challenges

Transition House struggled to find leadership and an identity that fit its mission, the current economic/demographic realities, and its organizational needs. Between 2004 and 2008 there was a succession of EDs, each serving for a year or less: three appointed "interim directors," one individual who was hired as ED, and one pair who were hired to split the job. The leadership was in turmoil, and the board struggled with a crisis of confidence about T House's identity. Fortunately, between 1998 and 2004 the staff had become much stronger, thanks to better structures and some excellent new hires, and the staff carried on. Long-term volunteers also continued to play a sustaining role through committees. The budget during this period was about $1 million, and the organization was again in financial crisis.

Interim Leadership and the Non-Merger with RESPOND, 2004 to 2005

Bill Stanton, hired by Elsbeth as a fund-raiser, offered to fill in as interim director. As might have been predicted, his appointment as interim director of this historic feminist organization immediately caused controversy. Long-time volunteers, supporters, and allies objected. A column in *Women's ENews* stated:

> Transition House, New England's first battered women's shelter, has always been known for its cutting edge work helping women and children escape abusive homes. Recently, however, the Boston-based, 30-year-old organization has set a precedent that makes some feminist activists uncomfortable. The board has not only hired a man as the interim executive director, but they are doing a gender-neutral search for a permanent hire set to conclude August 30th. About Women, a

collective of psychologists and social workers ... sees this as a step in the wrong direction. They wrote the board of Transition House a letter last October protesting what they called a "flagrant violation" of the organization's founding principles.[106]

In early 2005, the board hired Joyce King, a well-known African-American activist, feminist, and peacemaker to be part-time director of programs and services, and she took over the interim director title from Bill. Bill worked closely with Joyce and continued to handle the financial reporting and fund-raising side of the operation. As he saw it: they just had to "keep the ship afloat 'til we did a hire." Joyce was amazed "how bureaucratic and business-like" that ship had become. She observed, "They were counting everything; had rules and regulations." From her perspective, T House was no longer a feminist institution and had become part of the "non-profit industrial complex." Nonetheless, she oversaw the shelter and worked with Bill until fall 2005, when the next ED was hired. Joyce continued to fill an important stabilizing role through the changes of the next few years as a committee or board chair.

In July 2004, shortly after Elsbeth resigned, Transition House board members began meeting with board members of RESPOND to discuss the possibility of the two organizations merging. The interim ED and key board members felt that a merger might bring Transition House to a size that would allow for more professionalization and more financial stability. RESPOND needed more space, and T House needed more revenue to fully fund its existing programs and to grow. In addition, T House did not have an ED, so it seemed like an ideal time to consider a merger. In December 2004, the board hired a consultant to move merger discussions forward. For the next year a tremendous amount of board time and energy went into consideration of the merger.

By February 2005, board notes indicate, "The merger feels very probable right now, but is not definite." There was enough confidence about the likelihood of merger that this statement was given to the press: "Transition House, the oldest domestic violence shelter in New England and RESPOND, the region's first domestic violence agency have decided to go forward with plans to merge the two organizations ... Over the next five months the two organizations will proceed with a due diligence effort and plan to announce

---

106   Martin, C., "Violence Shelter Considers Hiring Male Director." *Women's ENews.* August 22, 2005. Retrieved from http://womensenews.org/story/domestic-violence/050822/violence-shelter-considers-hiring-male-director.

their decision in June, 2005."[107]

Among the perceived barriers were staff doubts and the two organizations' very different cultures, including differing definitions of domestic violence. Some also felt that T House did not have the strength to go into a merger as an equal, that the merger would be more like a takeover by RESPOND. However, in an e-mail, a board member wrote to both boards that "staff members were generally positive and understanding of our goal to create a larger and stronger agency that will be better positioned to serve the needs of victims of domestic violence, their families, and our communities."[108]

A long-term volunteer and board member expressed her opposition to the merger in a letter to the board in April 2005. She cited the importance of Transition House's history and the need to work on relationships in Cambridge, not merge with an organization strongly present in Somerville. She noted ongoing progress in diversity training and "a process of introspection and planning," which should be given time to continue before a merger can be objectively assessed.[109]

There were about 50 volunteers in 2005, many of whom were not in favor of the merger. A questionnaire given to the Volunteer Round Table in February asked: "What makes us special?" In response they wrote: "A. Transition House is unique in its ability to bring in volunteers. The agency appeals to people in the community because it is special. B. Our roots: Social activism, social justice, social change, grassroots and feminist. C. These differences in history and philosophy make us unique and that will be watered down if not lost in a merger." One volunteer wrote: "We are a symbol for the feminist, grassroots community."[110]

By April, the board was still moving forward, anticipating actual merger negotiations to take place in May. The board issued an e-mail to staff in which its members reported: "To efficiently design recruitment and hiring processes, the HR committees of both organizations will begin to work together to "fast track" the HR merger negotiations. The goal will be to draft an org chart and develop job descriptions for the merged version of senior management positions in the merged organizations, which each organization can use as the bases for the unmerged version." By necessity, the board was working on Plan A

---

107   Press release headed "RESPOND, Inc. and Transition House, Inc. Explore Plan to Combine Domestic Violence Organizations." January/February 2005.

108   Weenick, M. e-mail. February 3, 2005.

109   Bridger, F. Letter to the board. April 2005.

110   Notes. Volunteer roundtable. February 16, 2005.

(merger) and Plan B (non-merger) simultaneously.

The major explicit barrier repeatedly came down to "cultural differences" between the two organizations. RESPOND's criterion for entry, in effect their definition of domestic violence, was abuse by an intimate partner. T House had always had a more flexible approach, starting with the first person seeking refuge in the apartment, who had been abused by her son. Subsequently, the T House definition expanded to include many kinds of violence and threats against a woman that had not been anticipated in the founding days, e.g. threats of "honor killing" and experiences with trafficking.[111] RESPOND relied more strongly on therapy sessions for the women it served and required three counseling sessions for women entering shelter; T House focused on safety and support, maintaining a political power analysis of the issue, which implied a need for external changes. While T House had become more accepting of counseling and therapy for women dealing with trauma, they saw these services as supplementary and optional.[112] In addition, the RESPOND board was seen as less immersed in the issues of the field and the organization than the T House board.

The less-often mentioned issue, but possibly the ultimate deal breaker, was selection of an ED of a merged organization. RESPOND had an effective ED, a woman of color with a deep commitment to the issue of domestic violence. The RESPOND board apparently assumed that she would be the ED of a merged organization. The Transition House board assumed that there would be a search for an ED of the merged organization, in which the RESPOND ED could be a candidate. Somehow, these conflicting assumptions became clear only late in the process.

By May 2005, the board was still deep in discussion. The founding principles of T House were prominently on many board members' minds. This may have been a result of the situation: needing to think hard about organizational mission and vision. It may also have been affected by the particular membership of the board. In a memo of May 2005, the board stated the first pressing strategic issue with a potential merger is: "Our commitment to a radical grassroots empowerment model and our approach of engaging formerly battered women, their families, and the community in the development of our services should be preserved."[113] Later, the same document read: "Questions still remain. How do we get back to our grassroots? How do we once

---

111   April 2005 draft document to board, re: areas of strength and challenge in shelter program.

112   Ibid.

113   Opinion memo related to: Vision/Community, p. 1.

again become an organization that promotes collective responsibility for decision-making on the part of staff, volunteers and the board. Programs clearly need to be client centered and based on client needs, so how do we create a board that maintains input from the clients we serve and from staff and volunteers who run the programs."[114]

Key assets Transition House offered in a merger were seen as: "Our staff and volunteers; our history of innovative work in DV [domestic violence] prevention; a well-articulated vision based on feminist and womanist perspectives."[115] It is notable that in 2005 both volunteers and board members expressed such loyalty to the feminist perspective and "grassroots empowerment model" of T House. At the same time, many others saw these as already seriously compromised, if not long gone; still others, as obsolete or outgrown.

Without a clear consensus, the board committed to deciding whether they could be strongly pro-merger. A long-time volunteer, board member, and board chair presented compelling reasons to merge. These were:

1. Organizational stability.
2. Balance of administrative to program employees would tip to program side.
3. Greater breadth of service for both programs: RESPOND has support groups for women in community; Transition House has DVIP; RESPOND has more sustained legal advocacy program; Transition House has more housing programs. Difficult for either agency to start new programs without hurting old ones.
4. Greater fund-raising potential.
5. Building collaborations and more political power.[116]

On June 1, it was announced that "the boards of directors have determined that a merger at this particular moment does not appear to be an appropriate strategic choice, and we have closed our discussions."[117] This result was deeply disappointing to some, who had put a tremendous amount of time and effort into due diligence during that year. It was a great relief to others.

Leadership Issues, Who Are We?

As the search for a new ED moved forward, the T House board and staff met

---

114   Opinion memo related to: Vision/Community, p. 3.
115   Ibid.
116   Vielleux, N. Summary from May 5, 2005 meeting on merger.
117   Draft of announcement letter in merger binder.

to discuss the "qualities and talents for a new ED," to review the past year and to set goals and plans for the short-term. Although the merger was "off the table," RESPOND continued to share T House's shelter space, and efforts were made to improve the working relationships there. The board retreat notes from Summer 2005 mention the huge benefit of "great staff and volunteers. There's a lot of positive energy from the staff."[118]

There were (as always) challenges at the shelter. The August notes specify: the growing complexity of issues facing clients, for which there are no longer other services; the paucity of employment opportunities for clients; a need for a housing advocate at the shelter; a need to increase [staff] morale and help staff care for themselves; a need for more training on accessibility, given that T House had one of the few handicapped-accessible shelters.

The shelter director, trying to manage a difficult relationship between the two organizations sharing the shelter space, felt that, "the board was not leading. Lack of leadership was a big problem." Other programs also had specific challenges. The TLP needed a more comprehensive screening process. The housing shortage meant longer stays in transitional housing, and the inability to take undocumented women was a serious problem. T House still ambivalently served the Kent Street Apartments, a useful source of funds, but a poor fit with the mission.

The DVIP was working in nine schools. Schools were contributing more money than they had been, but funds were still insufficient. The program had become more clinical, working with kids from homes with the presence of domestic violence and/or who were experiencing violent relationships, sexual harassment, or anger management issues themselves.[119]

The volunteer program continued with a revised training manual and curriculum, and volunteer roundtables of five to 18 people met regularly until January 2006. The volunteer program was also underfunded, and the volunteer coordinator was doing too many jobs and feeling pressed to seek her own funds. A number of very long-term volunteers continued to be central to the staffing of the shelter; and their work at the shelter was important to them. One of them wrote in the Fall 2005 newsletter:

> These past 17 years at Transition House have been the best part of my life. I have had the opportunity to meet and get to know hundreds of women whose guts and resilience, tenacity and indomitable spirit

---

118   Organizational Retreat Notes, August 6, 2005, p. 2.

119   Ibid, p. 4.

have empowered them to overcome the crippling physical and mental abuse that came their way because someone became fanatically obsessed with controlling their lives. Because of their example, I am no longer ashamed, rather I consider myself a survivor, and I wear it like a badge of honor.[120]

With all the merger, staffing, governance, and financial issues, Transition House's presence in Cambridge had diminished. A staff person who began at T House in 2001 reported that "the first years there were lots of meetings in town. I was so proud to represent T House." Those meetings diminished, and by the time she left in 2006, "we never gained it back. So disappointing."

On the board, according to one of its members at the time, "There was a continuing thread of tension about the ED. Do we want one? What do we want from an ED?" Some board members were working to strengthen the staff leadership team, believing a new ED should respect and rely on that team. Other board members were focused on the ED search. Not surprisingly, the board's tensions affected the staff. One staff member recalled, "The board was not defining a vision ... There was a lack of principles and vision. Where are we going?" In the end, the announcement of the search for a new ED emphasized accountability to and communication with the board.

Norma Wassel, hired in the fall of 2005, began as full-time ED in January 2006. A seasoned clinician and administrator, Norma came into the ED role without a deep knowledge of T House's history. Financial stress was serious; the building again needed work (repairs to the foundation and dealing with rats in the basement); and staff was significantly stretched. In addition, the board was experiencing a big transition. The organization had just ended merger talks, and in the ensuing months almost half the board members left. Among those who left were key people who had helped the organization maintain some stability through many difficult years. On the staff side, the volunteer coordinator, one of the management team, also left. Unable to get funding for more outreach and more diversity work, she was discouraged and tired. "We were bouncing through a pinball machine of directors," she reflected, "without a coherent sense of purpose or history." Then in February 2006, the shelter director left. Looking back, she said, "I resigned because I was tired. The staff was great...[but] I never felt I did enough."

Coming in with fresh eyes, Norma questioned some of the long-time practices and beliefs. She wanted to examine the refusal to shelter women from

---

120   Doughty, W. Transition House newsletter, Fall 2005.

Cambridge and Somerville given the needed support of those towns; the ban on communication with abusers, given the complexity of experience of the women being served; the prioritizing of certain grants and services. The board, although depleted, still had members with a long T House history; the staff had strong views; the new ED was not given much room to make change. As Norma reflected: "I didn't expect the ED role to be so marginalized." And she added: "They were worn out already without taking all this on…. There was a resistance to challenging the status quo." A board member who came onto the board in 2003 observed that "they didn't really want [Norma] to be in charge of other people." By the end of the year, she resigned.

In the fall of 2006 a consultant's presentation to the board included the statements: "Let's be honest: Transition House's budgetary situation is in crisis;" and "In the short term, Transition House is grappling with a $200,000 budget deficit which must be filled by June, 2007, or the agency will close." The annual bare-bones budget was about $1 million, of which only 58 percent came from state funds. The consultants suggested that new sources of revenue were urgently needed to cover the deficit and recommended an aggressive fund-raising campaign to avoid the problem reoccurring next year.[121]

At the time of Norma's resignation, two board members, one white, one African-American served as co-chairs. They, in turn, looked to Joyce King as a mentor, valuing her history as an African-American feminist activist and former interim director. The tensions that had simmered in various ways for more than a decade were apparent. As one of the board leaders said, "There was a generational divide. The romantic era of Transition House was gone. It is a place that is expensive to run. … Are we an empowerment organization or a business?" A staff person articulated the same tension: "The roots were in a feminist concept of empowerment. Practices had shifted in ways some of which did not make sense. It wasn't really an empowerment agency and wasn't really a clinical agency."

In this context the board again considered the leadership question. Although there was a definite division of opinion on the board, the consensus was to hire two people, rather than one ED. One person would be a fund-raiser; the other, director of programs. The announcement of the positions read in part:

> The Director of Programs is responsible for overseeing and ensuring the effectiveness of the day-to-day operations of Transition House, including programs/services, staff management, and finances, and

---

121   Quoted or paraphrased from Carlisle & Company presentation to the Fund Development Committee.

community relations from a programmatic perspective.

The Director of Institutional Advancement is responsible for over-seeing and ensuring the effective long-term operations of Transition House, including fundraising, strategic thinking and planning and community relations from a fund development perspective.

Both Directors work in collaboration with one another, the Board of Directors and the staff within a participatory management model. In addition, both Directors will ensure quality, culturally-competent domestic violence services to the community.

Having twice experienced difficulties with EDs who lacked appreciation for the organization's history, the board selected someone as a co-director who was well known to board and staff from her prior work at Transition House. In fall 2007 Donna Kausek was hired as director of programs and Judy Andler as director of institutional advancement. The winter 2007 edition of the T House newsletter begins with their statement:

> This fall, we accepted the executive leadership of Transition House with anticipation and excitement. We are looking forward to meet-ing you and hearing from you. We look forward to sharing resources, expertise, and support as we build a community response to the needs of battered women. Our vision is to create the belief that a "violence free Cambridge" is a worthy goal, and that the process to attain it is valuable and necessary. We hope to generate excitement, investment and the will to make a meaningful and enduring difference for indi-vidual battered women and for the city.

Not long into the new co-directors' tenure, there were conflicts within the staff. Over the objections of some members, the board decided to meet with representatives of all groups to discuss the issues, as had been done in the collective years. A board member, who had been a volunteer for some years prior to joining the board, resigned. She felt that "[the board] made it too difficult for anyone to succeed in the executive role." One staff person, a person of color, was let go, after which several other people of color left. There were accusations of discrimination, and ultimately claims of the agen-cy's bias against a white employee. As in the late 1990s, issues of racism were seen as central to the conflicts.

Reflecting on that period, a staff member reported: "No one knew what was going on. When the co-EDs were hired ...we were already in deep financial trouble. I've thought many times we will have to close up. Then it was a very difficult time when [one staff member] left, and [another] marched out. Residents must have noticed the exodus of staff." From her point of view, in those years "the board was meddling or absent; no in-between." From the board's perspective, its members covered for the absent ED by taking on extra responsibilities, and expressed their care for the staff's perspective by including a staff representative (as well as a former client and the new head of the Women's Commission) on the hiring committee.

By the Spring of 2008 both co-directors had left. Transition House was again without an ED, having gone through an impressive number of EDs in the preceding four years.

CHAPTER 6

2008 to 2014: Finding a New Equilibrium

I n 2007-2008 the entire country faced a major recession, from which it was slow to recover. Unemployment went up; jobs were hard to find even for those with a good education and skills. Government-funded safety net programs were cut; private and foundation giving went down. Social service agencies of all sorts were struggling with decreased funding and decreased donations. Housing costs, which went down in many parts of the country, remained stubbornly high in Cambridge and greater Boston. The homeless population increased; shelter beds were full everywhere; affordable permanent housing was scarce anywhere near Boston. Emergency shelters essentially became a fiction, as there were often no emergency beds. The three-month limit on stays in emergency shelter, set by the state, was eliminated, given the reality that residents could not find post-shelter housing. Unable to find permanent housing, people moved from shelter to shelter. Those seeking refuge at the T House shelter were most often coming from another shelter, rather than directly fleeing a violent situation.

Although the recession technically ended in 2009,[122] the situation of people without assets did not improve in the second decade of the 2000s. National policies had become increasingly regressive through most of the life of Transition House, and these policies had direct consequences for the organization and the people it served. Internally, however, T House gained strength and, as one interviewee noted, "pulled itself together" as an organization.

---

122   See: https://economix.blogs.nytimes.com/2010/09/20/the-recession-has-official-ly-ended/. Retrieved October 2017.

Regaining Equilibrium, 2008 to 2010

This period started out looking quite gloomy. Severe funding issues, two lawsuits, stressed staff, and uncertainty about the direction of the agency intertwined with serious doubts about what was needed in an ED. From 2008 to 2012 T House operated without an ED. With support from a management consultant and increasing commitment from a new board member, the board and the staff management team took on leadership roles, and the organization gained a new equilibrium. This is, of course, easier to say in hindsight than it was to do at the time.

In February 2008, shortly after losing the co-directors, the board hired Laurie Holmes as a consultant. She had been the founding director of a successful Boston-area domestic violence organization from 1998 until 2007 and had a strong background with economic development programs. Her charge was to empower the staff and provide guidance to the board. At about the same time Risa Mednick, a long-time Cambridge resident, new to Transition House, joined the board.

In Laurie's understanding, "There was tremendous strength in the staff and a mess left behind from the former EDs." Also, "the bottom was falling out of the economy, and Transition House's reputation did not lead to more dollars." Laurie worked with the staff members on developing their skills to run the organization and with the board members to strengthen their leadership. She argued for more consistent input from residents, more community involvement, and a more accessible office. Recognizing the need for ongoing attention to issues of racism, she supported the beginning of a Boston-area Women of Color Network for those working against domestic violence and a group of Aspiring White Allies.

Her report five months later (June 2008) reads in part:

> Consecutive episodes of executive and board turnover over several years eroded organizational stability to such an extent that it raised credible worries about organizational collapse. A pattern emerged wherein some newly recruited staff and board quickly came to their assessment of the situation, freaked out, and jumped ship. Over and over again board members made well intended and noble efforts to quickly fill gaps and repair damage resulting from the void in consistent accountable leadership.... It is no wonder that so many burnt out or simply left. Another unintended consequence that occurred over time, and has perhaps been less readily apparent, is a slow erosion in organizational identity, culture and purpose.[123]

---

123   Laurie Holmes's report February-June 2008, p. 1.

That summer the board had to face the dire financial situation. They were about to move the administrative office to a larger but cheaper site and hoped to offer a new range of community-based services. The 2008-09 publicity for fund-raising emphasized the new focus on community partnerships. In a briefing document addressed to stakeholders, the board explained, "To provide more resources that survivors want and need, Transition House is expanding and launching its *Community Based Services program*. In collaboration with valued community partners, Transition House will offer a comprehensive array of services to families affected by violence." By the fall, and with the recession clearly evident, there were no grants to support these changes, nor was there enough money to maintain the consulting relationship with Laurie, which had been an additional burden on the strained budget.

The board decided to postpone searching for a new ED, basically to save money, but its members must also have been daunted by their poor hiring track record. Board and staff felt confident they could manage the organization effectively, although some funders expressed doubt. In Risa's view, "We had an executive management team with the necessary skills, and a hands-on board truly leading the institution." Many of the board members had been staff or volunteers earlier and had a "soul connection" to the organization. "That connection," she said, "got us through the lean years." In 2009 and 2010, there was again discussion of a merger—this time with the YWCA-Cambridge. This idea was explored very briefly and then abandoned by the boards of both organizations.

During Risa's first years on the board, she said, "I was learning a lot about not just Transition House, but how to run an organization, how to navigate broken systems while serving people responsibly, and to hold and revisit a mission." When her employment situation changed, and she had more time, "I became the de facto public voice of Transition House."

The staff, in 2008, was feeling the strain. Ester Serra Luque, who began as a case manager that year, reports that for her first couple of years, "We were very dependent on individual people who worked there because of the lack of central policies. Everyone felt overworked and had no time for anything else." There was also a lot of anxiety about the organization's financial state.

By 2010 Risa was working more intensively with the staff, and, as Ester noted, "Conversations started about policies and vision; everyone was wondering." There was, probably for the second time, a decisive turn toward the new. Internally, the management team, with Risa, clarified staff roles, routines, and processes. The already diminished role of community volunteers in staffing the agency became even smaller. The shelter, DVIP and non-emergency housing programs had been quite separate, but now staff roles were restructured to integrate the programs into one conversation and purpose.

Stability and Outreach, 2010 to 2014

New programs, new relationships, and collaborations characterized the period from 2010 to 2014. Staff morale was high, and community relations expanded and deepened. At the same time, a few long-time members of the Transition House community who had played important roles in its survival and success felt betrayed by the direction the organization was going, reflecting a lingering tension between the founding vision of the 1970s and the realities of the 2000s.

In 2011 the management staff was realigned to further integrate the shelter and other programs. The new positions were: director of housing programs, director of support services and community partnerships, director of youth and family programs, and ED. The management team was notable both for its diversity (including Muslim, Christian, and Jewish members; those of European and African descent; and those who were immigrants as well as those born in the United States) and its strong attachment and loyalty to each other and to T House. There were eight full-time staff members and 25 staff people altogether, comprising 17 full-time employees. The staff had an impressive range of cultural and linguistic fluency, including immigrants from Israel, Catalonia, Venezuela, Puerto Rico, Ethiopia, Haiti, and Iran. At least three employees were themselves survivors of domestic violence; one, a former TLP client.

The feeling reported by many staff people of being overburdened and uncertain about priorities and policies had abated. Continuing her reflections on the changes, Ester reported in 2014: "For the last three years we have been going down a path. We are still working things out, but have routines, policies, conversations." Much had been clarified, and the staff certainly appeared to be a well-functioning team.

Full-time staff people were very aware of the need to take care of themselves and each other to sustain the work. In part this reflects the whole field's increased awareness of secondary trauma, burnout, and need for self-care. In part, it may reflect the staff members' humbler sense of their own role than was characteristic of their early predecessors, and a greater sense of the complexity of survivors' needs. A number of staff people talked about learning to set personal boundaries, e.g. not being available by cell phone 24/7. Many mentioned learning to avoid a "fixing complex." Jasmine Khalfani, the director of housing, expressed this succinctly: "Staff has to understand they can't fix everything. Try to fix everything, and you end up disabling." A related theme concerned "empowerment." Long a central concept in domestic violence work, the T House staff continued—and continues—questioning its meaning. Societal systems (employment, education, housing, day care, welfare, immigration) are so "broken," "rigged," or "purposely designed to defeat poor people" (depending on the staff person's perspective) that "empowering" may be too grandiose. They talked in terms of "enabling," by supporting the survivor to develop skills and locate resources, helping her find and use her abilities; as opposed to "disabling," by doing too much for the survivor.

Staff morale was high, with a clear sense of colleagueship and shared purpose. Given the early fears of hierarchy, and the many years of difficulty dealing with a traditionally structured organization, the climate was especially notable. One staff member described the organization as "very flat. Everyone does everything. You don't feel that sense of hierarchy. Everyone is approachable; people don't feel they have to hide feelings, can talk openly with their supervisors and each other." According to another, "[I have] no gripes about the staff. This is one of the most supportive staffs I've ever worked with. It is very different, and it works." Yet another: "The teamwork, I don't even know how to describe it. We are like a big web."

In 2012 the board made Risa's role official (and paid) by choosing her as the next ED, continuing a new chapter for the organization with a more coherent identity and stable governance. Between 2012 and 2014 the board consisted of mostly new members. For the first time, it had no members "from within the ranks." In contrast to the very "hands-on" boards of earlier years, this one seemed to be fairly invisible to staff, although in Risa's view, "the board [came] through when needed."

The staff, including dedicated people who have been with T House for many years and through many changes, had been crucial to Transition House's survival. Reflecting on those last few years, Risa noted: "It is the grit of the staff that has made it all happen. They are smart, committed, skilled and talented."

As of 2014, the shelter is no longer a women-only space. Government funding requires that emergency shelters not discriminate against male victims, which became clear around 2009 or 2010, and the staff had to change "how [we] construed who our clients *might* be." Male victims can now seek refuge at Transition House, and there are sometimes male staff. Shelter residents have included a transgender woman, as well as straight and gay men. In reality, so few men seek services that the impact is small. One male staff member reflected: "In the shelter you need a special personality to be trusted, given what the women have been through." No one currently involved seems to see the loss of female-only space as a problem.

In 2009 the Department of Children and Families (DCF), formerly DSS, lifted the three-month limit on emergency shelter stays, a limit that for some time had been recognized as not realistic for finding housing. As the housing advocate reported: "It used to be easier in 2002. It gradually got harder around 2005-2006. The housing is not there." She went on to say that she always told the women to be hopeful; "if you go to the appointments and fill out all the applications, you should get housing in three years." That is what hope looked like in 2014: If a resident went to lots of appointments and filled out lots of forms, she was still likely to move around in temporary spaces for three years. Sustaining hope through years of shelter hopping, borrowed beds, kids changing schools and day care facilities cannot be easy. In addition, the housing one gets after years of trying may not be a good, or even appropriate, fit. (See Fatimah's story below.)

The lifting of the three-month limit was significant. It allowed time for deeper relationships among clients and staff. Many staff members noted that their earlier frustration with the very limited amount of time had been relieved. As one reported, "We get to know people incredibly well. We see children grow up, women complete college and get jobs. The longer they are in contact with us, the better they fare. With the shorter stay, just as they trust us and get services, they had to move on."

However, significant drawbacks to the lifting of the three-month limit existed. Beds were frequently not available when urgently needed for those seeking emergency shelter. A caller to the state hotline or the T House hotline was likely to be instructed to keep calling back, in the hope that a call will coincide with an open bed. Emergency shelter had, essentially, become a fiction in the state. While the T House shelter was able to do much more with and for the women housed there, it could not often do what it was created to do: provide an immediate refuge for those fleeing violence.

In 2014, the residents in the shelter were "as culturally diverse as any group can be," but economically similar. Almost none had any meaningful financial resources. Most were under age 30, but there were also women over 50. Most had little education. More and more had been without stable housing for at least five years, and most women had been in other shelters before coming to Transition House. "To have a first shelter experience at Transition House [was] very unusual," Risa noted. "It's no longer a woman fleeing in dead of night with a backpack." With the longer stays relationships developed and stuff accumulated. A client who moved out with her baby after about a year needed a mover.

Perhaps because of the residents' longer stays and/or the stable and well-functioning staff, the rules governing the residents in the shelter were re-considered and, in some ways, relaxed. In the continual struggle for a shelter culture that is neither punitive nor chaotic, it seemed possible to be less controlling without risking safety. An overnight staff person who had worked at T House for 13 years believed the changes were very positive. This person said, "People used to get warnings for cooking at night after 8 PM. There were too many rules. It's changed. There are fewer rules; a friendlier atmosphere … The mood is better."

Transition House ended its work with the Kent Street housing program in 2013. The TLP continued to support for up to two years nine individuals and families in four scattered sites. Seven units of permanent supported housing were available to domestic violence survivors with a concurrent documented disability. Those residents continued to apply for housing and could get sustainable funding through Social Security Disability Insurance. Once they had the resources, they could take over the lease for the unit from Transition House, in which case Transition House would rent another unit, or the resident could leave and rent elsewhere. The turnover was usually three to five years. From 2012-2015 Transition House collaborated with the Gay Men's Domestic Violence Project to provide one additional unit of Permanent Supported Housing to one of their clients.

The DVIP lost funding in 2009 and discontinued counseling in schools, work that was anyway running into barriers. With pressure from the Massachusetts Comprehensive Assessment System exams, less in-school time was available for non-academic activities. Also, as the DVIP work had gotten more clinical, there was concern about legal and ethical issues. When did DVIP staff need parental permission to speak with students? Were DVIP staff/interns in sufficiently clinical roles that they needed licensure? Julie Kahn-Schaye who had directed the DVIP since 2006 moved to a job in the shelter, while continuing to facilitate groups, train, and supervise work in the schools. She became the first full-time licensed social worker employed in-house, part of the management team, and available to residents for voluntary therapy.

As the in-school DVIP program shrank, the Youth Action Corps (YAC) developed. It began as a six-week summer program with student participants paid through the Mayor's Summer Youth Employment Program. In 2012, the YAC received a three-year grant to become a year-round after-school and summer leadership development program. The program included eight to 10 male and female students between 14 and 18 years old, all of whom were paid. It was designed to "train peer leaders on healthy relationships to train others in their community." YAC members reflected with staff on relationship issues, including religious and cultural norms. They developed skills, e.g. at participating in meetings; leading workshops for other students, parents, and schools; and speaking in public. Asked whether she deemed gender an important issue in dating violence, the YAC facilitator responded: "It is everyone's issue, how someone treats someone else, defying gender."

As leadership became stronger and the staff management team more integrated, T House was able to move forward with more community connections, as had been planned earlier. In 2009 Transition House became a founding member of the Cambridge, Arlington, Belmont High Risk Team (CABHART), joining with the Guidance Center, Inc. (specifically its program for children who witness violence) and the police chiefs of the three towns. This team identified families at risk for lethal domestic violence and provided individualized support to those families.

The same year T House began offering stabilization services to program participants leaving for permanent housing in the Greater Boston area, i.e. ongoing work in the community with families formerly in T House housing. In 2013 the Cambridge Housing Authority (CHA) began support for a community liaison to work with families in public housing who may or may not have used other T House services. This was a big step in providing support and resources to people dealing with domestic violence who were not homeless and had not already sought services. The community liaison also met with a support group of women, most referred by other agencies, who do crafts and activities once a week at the T House office. A young woman in the community who fled an abusive situation was referred to the liaison. After they got to know each other, the liaison invited the young woman to the group meeting. The rest of the women were between 30 and 60 years old; even the youngest was older than the newcomer. As reported by the community liaison, the client got a lot of information from the group and a new perspective on her situation. The young woman realized, "All of you [in the support group] went through this too. I thought I was just stupid." In the recent past, the ideals of the founders of Transition House—of peer help and women empowering women, have not faded entirely into memory.

During these years, Transition House developed new relationships with the city council, the city manager, and with related Cambridge nonprofit agencies

(Emerge, Community Legal Services and Counseling Center, The Guidance Center Inc., Cambridge Health Alliance, and CHA). In 2012 T House became affiliated with the Gay Lesbian Bisexual Transgender Domestic Violence Coalition.

Most volunteers at Transition House worked with the children at the shelter and came through Horizons for Homeless Children, an agency that trains and places volunteers at many shelters. T House was a desired placement, according to the T House staff person who supervised the volunteers, because "there are fewer issues than elsewhere." About 30 volunteers worked in two-hour shifts with at least a six-month commitment. They were trained for one day by Horizons and had a supplementary training of two hours at T House focusing on children who witness/live with domestic violence.

Applying for grants and anxiety about funding were constant burdens. At least as troubling, funders' requirements were often not a good fit with the actual needs of Transition House residents and other clients. In this, Transition House was not alone; it is a widespread complaint of grant-dependent non-profits. Funders often want to see evidence of clients' "progress," as defined by the funding organization. This setting of goals from "above" violated the early concept of empowerment and even the current idea of enabling clients to find and use resources (their own and externally). The outcomes funders seek simply do not always line up with reality. Attention to those outcomes can also, as one respondent said, "separate you from those you try to help," whose personal desired outcomes may be quite different.

In 2010, as Risa was emerging in a leadership role on the Transition House board and working with the staff, Marjorie Decker, a Cambridge City councilor, came for a visit. The visit was encouraged by Nancy Ryan, the retired long-time head of the Cambridge Women's Commission. Although frustrated with the organization's "bunker mentality" in the 1980s, Nancy had been a consistent ally of Transition House over the years. Marjorie grew up in Cambridge and remembered the city-wide domestic violence initiative of the 1990s, which was active when she was finishing college. Known as the Domestic Violence Free Zone (DVFZ), that initiative was spearheaded by Katherine Triantifillou who was a city councilor in 1995 and had been the first lawyer working with Transition House back in the 1970s. Community collaboration on domestic violence had diminished in the 15 years since the DVFZ as resources had gotten scarcer, and attention to domestic violence had flagged. Marjorie agreed to help bring "more people to the table." From the beginning she had important allies, including the city manager and assistant city manager.[124] But there was also some resistance. "I didn't fully understand [about] challenging silos," she said recently.

In the fall of 2011, with many organizational allies, Marjorie organized a "domestic violence summit" for Cambridge. That very large gathering led to a working group which met to develop a plan. In collaboration with a group at MIT they launched a "question campaign" in 2012 to gain wide community input and increase visibility of the issue of domestic violence.[125] Ultimately, the working group created a proposal for a paid position to head a "Domestic and Gender-based Violence Prevention Initiative," hereafter referred to as the Prevention Initiative. The city manager agreed to fund this position, which would report directly to his office. The position was filled in Fall 2014 by Elizabeth (Liz) Speakman, MSW.

---

124   Cambridge has a Plan E form of government, which has a strong city manager. The city manager is the city administrator and is appointed by the city council. The city council is elected and chooses a mayor from among the city councilors.

125   The publicity for that campaign, including some history of domestic violence initiatives in Cambridge, is available at (https://www.cambridgema.gov/~/media/Files/citymanagersof-fice/dvfolder/ReportFINAL-(3).pdf).

CHAPTER 7
2014 to Present: Evolving New Strategies and Partnerships

By 2014 Transition House had emerged from a period of organizational struggle over leadership and finances. Risa had officially become the ED; the board and staff had stabilized the organization's finances; and for the first time since the earliest years, governance was apparently not a contentious issue. Work was in process to renovate the shelter building (completed in 2015), and, even with that project underway, the housing programs were running well. In that context, the board and staff agreed to direct the agency's attention outward into the community, and they nurtured new relationships there. That process led over the next few years to dramatically changed relationships between Transition House and the city and to new ways of enacting the mission to respond to and prevent domestic violence. Transition House's current activities express and reflect an explicit and expanded social justice agenda.

Transition House has implemented community-based services, which had not been feasible when envisioned back in 2008 and 2009. It became feasible because the agency had weathered leadership changes and the recession and had made a concerted effort to develop relationships with allied (and potentially allied) departments and agencies in Cambridge. The city's renewed engagement, growing out of the city-wide efforts since 2011, was also critical. In the same period, new state funding resources became available to realize new goals.

Transition House's new chapter is built on the recognition that most survivors of domestic violence are living in the community—not only because shelter is rarely available, but also because they prefer it. It is also based on a conception of domestic violence as an issue that the community needs to "own" and that is deeply connected to other forms of oppression and, therefore, to other community concerns. Relationships in the community are seen as key to response and prevention, and prevention is the path to ending domestic violence. My account focuses on the newer aspects of Transition House, as the shelter and housing programs have been discussed in earlier chapters. It is again based on interviews and influenced now also by my own observation. The current organizational chart gives an overview. (Figure 7: Organization chart 2017.)

Community Outreach and Connections

The Domestic and Gender-Based Violence Prevention Initiative[126] under Liz Speakman's leadership, is a key partner to Transition House; and Transition House staff are important members of the Prevention Initiative's steering committee and working groups. The executive committee to which Liz reports includes the directors of major city departments, which keeps these important city officers informed about and aware of domestic and gender-based violence issues and how the city can best address them.

The fact that the director of the Prevention Initiative reports directly to the city manager's office conveys the city's commitment to the issue of domestic and gender-based violence and facilitates the Prevention Initiative's access to city systems. Some city systems have quickly formed productive partnerships with the Initiative based largely, Liz believes, on relationships those systems already had with Transition House. These include notably, the Cambridge Police Department (CPD) and the Cambridge Housing Authority (CHA). Other city departments, which are important for the work of violence prevention, such as the Cambridge Public Schools and the Cambridge Health Alliance, are in earlier stages of forming relationships with the Prevention Initiative. Liz works with Transition House to provide training throughout the city. The entire police department, including civilian staff and new officers, has had domestic violence training, as have all employees of the Housing Authority. Transition House and the Prevention Initiative also brought specialized trauma training to the police department.

Reflecting on her job, Liz sees its core as ensuring more connectivity: "Cambridge has a lot of resources, but they are not always working collaboratively or going in the same direction. A big part is minimizing fragmentation, connecting silos. [It was] not the intention of the city, maybe, but a big part of the job has to be systems change." From Risa's point of view Transition House's partnership with the city's Prevention Initiative is a great asset: "It amplifies

---

126   For more information about this initiative, see https://www.cambridgema.gov/Departments/domesticandgenderbasedviolencepreventioninitiative.

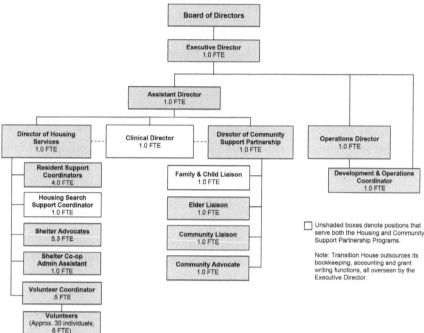

(Figure 7: Organization chart 2017.)

our work and puts theory into practice. For years, the DV [domestic violence] field has been trying to communicate that domestic violence is not an intractable social problem and whole communities must be part of the solution. In Cambridge, we can now test holistic community approaches to prevention and intervention with partners from different disciplines and sectors. More people and organizations are joining in this effort, in part because it has the imprimatur of our city's leadership."

In 2014 there was one community worker at Transition House, funded by the CHA and dedicated to working with people in public housing, applicants to public housing and Housing Authority staff. When Liz began her job she quickly allied with the Transition House objective of increasing community work, believing that, "The local domestic violence agency has to be at the center of work in the community." "When I started I knew there weren't [sufficient] community-based services through Transition House. I knew I needed to be able to refer to services to do this job ethically. So, I advocated with the city … so that Transition House could build up their capacity." At the same time the high-risk team (a partnership, which includes Transition House, the police and the Guidance Center) needed leadership. Working together, the Prevention Initiative, Transition House, CPD and the CHA agreed on a new position to be funded by the city and the CHA. That person would provide counseling and advocacy in the community at large as well as leadership for the high-risk team. Subsequently, Transition House got funds from the Massachusetts Office of Victim Assistance (MOVA) for a new clinical/counseling position for community work. More recently MOVA has also funded a children's advocate for the team. In the last two years, the community team has gone from one member to a team of four. Liz says, "I could not do my job without that team. Not just the team, but who they are."

The Community Support Partnership is led by Ester Serra Luque, who has been at Transition House since 2008. "The name is a reflection of the intention behind it," she says. "Domestic violence is not only Transition House's problem." Ester reports that during the first year of partnership with the CHA, when she was the only community worker, she saw more than 80 families, which proved the need. "And there is a huge prevention piece of it that we are interested in, not just dealing with emergencies. We need to go back to infusing ourselves in the community, doing things more long term to address root causes."

The team collaborates and partners with many Cambridge organizations. While Emerge and Transition House have always been connected, their work together on youth programs and community trainings has increased recently. The Boston Area Rape Crisis Center is also a partner; for instance, on summer youth workshops. Cambridge's Community Legal Services and Counseling Center now has an attorney at Transition House's office one day a week for consultation with clients and staff. The Cambridge Economic Opportunity Committee helps with financial literacy workshops and financial consultation. Transition House's community advocate, Valerie Druckenmiller, has walk-in hours at the CHA. Members of the team participate in many community meetings beyond these partner agencies and do trainings for all kinds of programs and groups.

Describing her work, Valerie says, "We [do] a lot of outreach to agencies in the community to build relationships. So they call us when they meet with someone and something comes up [relating to domestic violence]. People call to talk through the situation or to refer a client. A big one is the Cambridge Police Department. I work a lot with their domestic violence liaison, Alyssa

Donovan, and follow up on every domestic violence report. Also a lot of clients are court involved, and she can help me with that." One long term goal, Valerie notes, is that these systems be more trauma informed.

Valerie has two business cards. One has the organization logo and the usual information; the other has her title "community advocate," her cell phone number and a generic e-mail address. Transition House and domestic violence are not mentioned on that card. The intention is to convey resource information in a way that is inviting to people who need support and who may not label themselves as domestic violence victims. That card also will be less likely to trigger suspicion if it is found by a volatile partner. When Valerie gets a call she explains what she can and cannot do and the limits of confidentiality and then tries to figure out what is needed and to help the caller find it. "The only one-time phone calls are from other towns," she says. A lot of her time goes to housing and legal issues and to the clients of the high-risk team. "I work with people in crisis, and usually they resurface at some point," she adds. "I have been working with some of them as long as I've been here."

The third member of the team, since Summer 2015, is Shameka Gregory, whose title is community liaison. With the rest of the team she does outreach to agencies and trainings, and she is specifically focused on outreach to the faith community. Trained as a clinical social worker, she facilitates weekly groups for survivors, provides one-on-one counseling weekly or as needed, and does individual advocacy. "Here it's about the client and what they need and finding a way to make it happen; just getting it done. I love the work, the mix of things," says Shameka.

The newest member of the team is Venus Taylor, who started in Fall 2016. She is specifically the child and family liaison, a position that evolves in response to the need. "I get to do all that I like: parent-groups, teaching and training and presenting, direct work with families and couples, and no insurance stuff and paperwork." "It's always about healing, intergenerational healing. Secondarily, [it's about] fostering more trauma-informed and trauma-sensitive environments especially for kids." She adds: "We do a lot more that the materials don't communicate. The gay/trans work—we do a lot of that … A lot of 'know your rights,' supporting immigrants, especially in this political climate."

Ronit Barkai, the assistant director of Transition House, has been an anchor on the staff since 2002 and one of the sources of its resilience. She was instrumental in designing and continues to guide the management of the Community Support Partnership. Reflecting on the organization's new priorities she says, "We were focused primarily on crisis management until about

2012." "Since then, we have learned management strategies that make our work more effective and our organization stronger. We knew we had to have a community-focused program, and now we do." She is particularly passionate about developing culturally specific outreach and support options, currently planned for Latina and Bangladeshi women. The leaders of these groups are members of the Cambridge Community Engagement Team (CET)[127] who got to know Transition House through their work on the steering committee of the Prevention Initiative. Transition House also participates in the development and facilitation of CET's *Making Connections* training program for Cambridge on community engagement.

Maria Chavez has been on the CET since early 2014. When the Prevention Initiative sought members from the CET, Maria volunteered. From the Dominican Republic herself, she connects with immigrants from many Spanish-speaking cultures. "I learn in my job from the other cultures." In addition to participating in the steering committee and outreach working group of the Prevention Initiative, Maria has participated in trainings and conferences as well as "know your rights" workshops on which Transition House collaborates. Maria's work illustrates the need to address many issues of oppression simultaneously. She notes her concern now especially for undocumented immigrants. "How can people feel safe to go to police or get help? Things are changed in how I need to do my job now. I feel the mistrust. [People may think] 'you work for immigration [because you work for] the city.'" Her job has gotten broader. "People in crisis call and cry. People are packing to go back [to their home countries]. I have a list of resources from 'know your rights.' I try to give people places that are certified, where there is no fraud. I do what I can to alleviate the situation and also spread the word about the Latina support group, but now people are worried about whether they are safe in this *country* more than [whether they are safe from abuse] at home." Of Transition House she says, "I feel proud to be here. Being part of this place is powerful."

The Community Support Partnership and the Domestic and Gender-based Violence Prevention Initiative are both anchored tightly to or completely part of Transition House. They are intrinsic to, but certainly not the full extent of, Transition House's current community partnerships. Risa describes the effort to partner with outside entities: "Part of the organizational operational dimension is about creating resources within the organization to have the strength

---

127   The Community Engagement Team hires and trains immigrant Cambridge residents to engage and assist underserved families in their communities. See https://www.cambridgema. gov/DHSP/programsforadults/communityengagementteam.

to be a good partner to the outside. Having the ability to not just manage the crises within, but think in a more creative way about what possibilities exist to fulfill our mission and who our natural and less obvious partners are. That has been an accomplishment." "How you assess who is a good partner is interesting…You have to gauge strategically where the opportunity and will for effective change is." Among the strong partnerships are three described in the next sections.

New Kinds of Partnerships

Susan Pacheco has been the director of the Council on Aging since 2012 and part of the agency for much longer. She says she has been "beating the drum about elders and abuse" since the late 1990s, but the focus in the domestic violence world was always on younger people. In about 2013, Ronit contacted her because Transition House was seeing more seniors. "I met with Ronit and Risa, and I have been there ever since. We made this incredible connection … They were finally catching up." "Having that relationship with them, I am just beyond impressed. Five years ago I would not be at the table. Now it's my table."

The partnership began with in-service training on domestic violence for the Council on Aging staff. In 2014 a Cambridge Elder Abuse Prevention Initiative started meeting monthly including Greater Boston Legal Services, as well as the police, district attorney's office, protective service of Somerville-Cambridge Elder Services, the Prevention Initiative, and others. The group enables consultations, expanded resources, and "warm handoffs," when referrals are made. "The silos are broken," Susan says with enthusiasm, "there are no wrong doors" for getting help.

On the basis of this coalition Transition House and the Council on Aging received a grant from the Tufts Health Plan Foundation to address elder abuse, which supports training, outreach and direct services. A training was held in May 2017, bringing together providers working with elders and those working in domestic violence/sexual assault agencies. Support groups for elders at the Cambridge Senior Center and at the Massachusetts Association of Portuguese Speakers are next on the agenda.

"Unlike many organizations in the field, we have had some really excellent traction with law enforcement in Cambridge and see our Police Department as a partner in the realm of community culture change," Risa notes. "This is exciting and strategically very important because it means that the way police understand domestic and sexual violence is changing. Officers and policy makers can both hold the notion that they are addressing a crime, but they are addressing the impact of trauma at the same time. It extends beyond the Domestic Violence and Sexual Assault unit itself. Increasingly, local police see things through a different lens and seek out resources in a different way in order to help people."

Within the CPD, Joanne McEachern, reflects on change in the relation between Transition House and the CPD in the last couple of years. She has been a police officer for 24 years, 12 of them on the domestic violence unit. "Initially, the relationship between Transition House and the police was not a great coordination," she says. "Both were a little leery. There is a trust there now. We do trainings together a lot. Both are working for the same thing, to keep survivors safe so they can continue to thrive." "We didn't understand before how much [survivors] were being triggered. Now I understand why they are being vague. I understand where Transition House is coming from. Also, they understand the police more. Used to be they'd call and just ask for a car. Now we know each other." She does safety training with survivors and a self-defense class with a partner from Transition House who also translates as needed.

"With the CPD," Liz says, "I have seen a real shift in how some understand what survivors go through. I hope that was translated into how they interact. That's probably where most impact is in terms of systems change." When asked how she envisions systems change, she responds, "Initially through training to building relationships of trust and credibility, and also getting a better sense of the needs of the system." Recently, she had a conversation with an officer about an incident. "He has referenced the conversation as challenging, but useful. Our relationship allowed it. That's how it happens: relationship leads to trust, and then hard conversations don't destroy the relationship."

The CHA has had an ongoing relationship with Transition House through voucher programs for rental housing and a program for emergency housing (people with immediate need due to sudden loss of housing from fire, flood, unsafe conditions, or fleeing domestic violence, for instance). The emergency housing program always has a wait list. Shayla Simmons is an attorney in the legal department of the CHA and about five years ago was part of a meeting with Transition House to brainstorm about the emergency status process. CHA was hoping Transition House would take it over. Instead, Transition House asked for a different approach altogether: actual units in CHA housing, not vouchers. Thus began the "pathways to permanent housing program" and a relationship that allowed for thinking together about other ways to partner.

Fifty percent of the calls from CHA properties to the police are for domestic incidents, according to Shayla, suggesting the need for more accessible education and resources for residents. Transition House did presentations for the Housing Authority departments and subsequently began walk-in hours for staff and residents in CHA buildings. Ultimately, CHA committed its financial support for the first Community Partnership Team member. "Once we had a dedicated community person, the demand increased," Shayla notes, which led to the decision to train all CHA staff.

Shayla's reflections on the domestic violence training speak to its impact: "It was awesome, a great experience. Their ability to tailor the training to our specific needs was what made it fantastic." Shayla continues: "It not only impacted our work. It changed the level of conversation in the office…[our staff is] more sensitive to domestic violence, open to talking with each other." As intended, the relationship with Transition House's community team, has improved their ability to help survivors of domestic violence. When a CHA employee meets with a survivor of domestic violence, "it is such a relief to refer to a person who can come to them. It has really raised the bar on our service." Even when there is no emergency housing available, there can be help through Transition House. The community team can respond to situations that are not emergencies, as residents and staff seek advice about personal situations or consultation about situations they hear of or observe. System-wide from front desk staff to maintenance workers, who are in and out of apartments all day, CHA employees have called for consultation and offered intervention support with Transition House.

Changes in the Housing Programs and Staff

Within the shelter, Transition House has fewer rules and more relaxed requirements than at any time in the recent past. State funding moved last year from the DCF to the Department of Public Health with some changes in funding requirements based on research with survivors and providers, and these changes are very much in line with the direction of Transition House. For instance, services cannot be required for shelter residents. Ronit recounts: "It is never just domestic violence for our clients. If you are intoxicated, that does not mean we can't house you …We'll offer options to support sobriety and stress reduction. We encourage conversation to alleviate shaming. Survivors of domestic and sexual violence endure enough shame."

Even before the Trump administration, federal priorities were shifting funding away from transitional models to permanent housing, with emphasis on chronically homeless and disabled people. In response, Transition House has expanded its permanent housing supply little by little. Extending its work with the CHA allows Transition House to access additional units for survivors who have been involved with its programs. As in its other supported housing models, the organization is the tenant of record for the first year, after which (if all goes well) the survivor is qualified to lease the unit. So far, 15 people have participated and secured a permanent home.

Domestic Violence in the Context of Systems of Oppression

In the last few years the management team of Transition House has made a consistent and concerted effort to recast Transition House as an anti-oppression agency. Ester states: "We want that to be the philosophy, domestic violence as a societal issue, an oppression issue, and we have to be aware of domestic violence as part of larger systems of oppression." According to Risa, "We aim to transform the way this community (with an eye on the bigger culture) understands and addresses issues of gender-based violence…. domestic violence is deeply rooted in systemic inequity and sexism and patriarchy. It is not about an individual pathology or relationship, but about the way society is organized. It helps to be in an organization with a political analysis—from the beginning." As Ronit puts it: "Everything connects. We are seeing people in the context of their whole lives, beyond domestic violence, struggling with poverty, legal issues, mental health, substance abuse, housing—oppressions of different sorts, all sorts. I hope we are seen as an anti-oppression agency, not an agency that is just about domestic violence."

This effort to shift the organization's culture and approach shapes hiring decisions and organizational policies and procedures. Ester says, "We want to hire people who understand how racism permeates and affects life of survivors differently, how your immigration status, gender identity, economic level— all these kinds of things how these are connected, and we as an organization and as individuals have different power positions and how we can be very mindful of these." Policies and procedures are being examined and altered to be consistent with this stance. Job descriptions and even interview questions have been revised to reflect this thinking and attract staff members who are committed to social change. Feedback from staff and clients informs planning.

Staff morale oddly echoes that of the early collective, and the sense of embarking on something new and exciting also feels reminiscent of the earlier agency. Many staff members expressed a sense of collective responsibility to each other and to the agency. There is a staff wellness program, and people support each other on wellness goals. Ronit expressed the general feeling: "If you need support we are here for you—clients and staff." Low staff turnover is also a testament.

Conclusion

Transition House began as a radical organization identified with a movement for social change while also providing services for those fleeing abuse. For decades Transition House resisted pressure to adopt a traditional governing structure and to hire mental health professionals, maintaining the collective and informal relations among volunteers, residents, and staff. As the political and economic context made the work of Transition House increasingly challenging, that loyalty to its founding principles may have contributed to the difficulties it finally faced in the mid-1990s. Ultimately, it lost its identification with a political movement, which had, itself, moved on. From the late 1990s until the early 2000s Transition House struggled with organizational and financial challenges, though it never wavered in its commitment to those it serves. In the last decade, and particularly in the last few years, it has emerged as a stronger organization with a renewed sense of mission that is again framed in terms of societal oppression and injustice, in what could be considered political terms. The liberation work today is not just about women and male power, but about those oppressed in many different ways by the inequities and injustices of our present society.

Transition House has, from the start, existed in the tension between its social service and social change missions. While the analysis of those leading Transition House today is a political analysis, the work is being done in close collaboration with the political and social service establishment of Cambridge, and that is a real difference from Transition House's early years. While not identified with a single social movement, the agency has a definite sense of movement into new territory. As Risa says, "We act on our mission in a whole different way." I will end this chapter with a quote from Ester: "I did not understand how social service agencies could do social change work when I started.... It's still a question, but the lines blur in a good way with this change in philosophy."

CHAPTER 8
Stories and Themes

In addition to Lynne, who came first to the apartment and then to the house on Elm Street, and Liz, who was a resident with her children in the 1980s, I was able to interview three recent clients, in each case of the TLP. They are women who have stayed in touch with T House and were willing and able to take the time to speak with me. Their stories below illustrate the realities women face after shelter, the persistence and courage demanded of them, and the role T House played.

Fatimah's Story

Fatimah's husband had been beating her for about 10 years before they immigrated from South Asia with their children to the United States in 2004. About a year later her husband was arrested for domestic violence, and she took out a restraining order against him. With new freedom to act, Fatimah began English as a Second Language (ESL) classes. However, the local immigrant community from their culture intervened, supporting him, and she tried again to make the marriage work. With little English and no permission from her husband to return to the ESL classes, she felt trapped.

In desperation Fatimah confided in a counselor at her children's school, who referred her to a shelter. Once housed there she resumed ESL classes and began a job search. Over the next year she and her children moved from a shelter to a Department of Transitional Assistance (DTA) supported motel room, spending some days also at the private home of the school counselor. In 2009, with a DTA referral, she applied for transitional housing at T House. Her daughter was in school in Boston, her young son was in day care, and one son was living with her estranged husband.

In Transition House's TLP Fatimah started college classes and a housing search. She reports that T House "helped me a lot with my education: parenting classes, finance classes, housing searches. Also finding friends, some other Muslims, one is on staff." She talked about the housing search and its results: "I applied for more than 100 housing. After a year I found a house in Everett. That was very hard. The house was on top of a hill. I had no car, don't drive. It was hard to shop and a half-hour walk to drop kids at school." Ultimately, Fatimah found more appropriate housing on her own. She remembers her Transition House advocate saying, "'You are brave.' She was happy I did everything myself. With this house, I am happy. For the first time since I got married."

Fatimah has found part-time work in her new town, and she has received an associate degree in accounting. Last summer she volunteered at the Transition House shelter. She finally divorced, became a US citizen, and brought her parents to the United States. Although she no longer needs housing services, Transition House continues to be part of her life, partly through the continuing relationships with staff, but also through continued practical help. She explains, "T House is still helping to finance my education, getting scholarships to go on."

Lucinda's Story

Lucinda immigrated from South America to the United States to go to college. Fleeing a violent husband, she went first to a hospital and then two Boston shelters. From there she got a space at Transition House's TLP, having already applied for permanent housing.

While a TLP resident, Lucinda was part of a staff/client committee to interview ED candidates in 2007. Wanting to work, she sought child care for her very young child, but the cost was discouraging. She lamented, "Affordable child-care is too hard. Women are punished for having a family. I had to pay [for child care], and it took most of my salary." Lucinda learned she could volunteer at T House and bring her son along, which she did. After a little over a year in the TLP Lucinda got a small apartment and then a larger one.

The week her son started preschool, Lucinda joined the Transition House paid staff. She asserted, "I love It ... They've been more than family to me." She even decided not to take another job with considerably more pay, saying, "I like the chaos. It's never routine. There is constant problem solving. They pay me to do what I like to do—[I have] a real purpose." She noted that for T House "money is always a challenge. It would be great to have some fund-raising."

Karla's Story

Karla immigrated from Central America in 2008. Four years later she fled to a shelter with her 18-month-old son. From there she got a space in the TLP. She remembers, "They gave me workshops, groups on domestic violence, how to get help if you want to study something." She got training to be a certified nursing assistant and found a job.

After 18 months Karla got Permanent Supported Housing in T House's program. If she gets a Section 8 voucher, she can use that to stay where she is or move. "One of my goals is to get independent of Section 8…I still talk with my advocate. She is still with me until one day I can try to be totally independent. I still need help from the lawyer and from her. I am in a better place than I was living before; made some good decisions for me and my son." Her son is now in preschool. "Living in shelter was hard for him. [I] saw he was very confused. Preschool changed him totally, in a good way. [He has] improved in so many ways. He's doing great. He's happy in that place." Still, his visitation with his father is hard: "It's hard to trust him [my son's father]. He's not focusing on [our son]." Sometimes her son beats on her and says, "My Daddy do that."

Ending the interview, Karla says,

> For me T House is like my second family here. In this country [I have] only my brother, and he couldn't help me much. [My son] doesn't know what T House is. But the T House staff are like family to him. When the office moved, he wanted to get back to the old office. It is a big important part of his life. It was hard for him to leave his home and his father. They helped him feel the connection. He says "hi" to all the people in the office by name. They work together with me and listen to me. Maybe because it is their job, but it's not just their job.

Recurring Themes
MOVEMENT ORGANIZATION AND/OR SERVICE ORGANIZATION

Transition House began as part of a larger national and local feminist movement. The founding women were clear that it was a movement organization, part of the women's movement of the 1970s. Its purpose was profound social change, not social service. As a movement organization, its fundamental principles were: women helping women (no professionals); a collective/ collaborative structure; and organizing to empower women, particularly women dealing with domestic violence. Over time, adhering to these ideals became problematic. Yet, the board of directors and staff maintained a strong loyalty to the founding principles. Devotion to the founding principles can be viewed as impeding progress, maintaining integrity, or both.

LEADERSHIP IN THE CONTEXT OF A MISTRUST OF POWER

Collective governance and a non-hierarchical structure were central to the Transition House narrative for decades. From the beginning it was difficult to run an organization with an ideology of equal voice for every participant, increasingly difficult as the organization became more complex, and finally, impossible. While the collective was a powerful medium for consciousness-raising and its participants felt empowered, it seems an impractical way to run a residential program for dislocated strangers in crisis who need a consistent and predictable temporary home.

It is a tribute to the commitment and endurance of the collective members that it worked as well as it did for as long as it did. At the same time, the profound distrust of hierarchical power became an organizational problem, which was difficult to resolve. The shift to a more traditional organizational structure and the trust in that structure happened over more than a decade and with ambivalence, but did definitely happen. The more recent staff and residents have been pleased with the leadership structure, which current staff members describe as non-hierarchical, although everyone acknowledges it is not a collective.

Perhaps it is not surprising that an organization whose central purpose concerns abuses of power is deeply ambivalent about power.

PEER HELP AND PROFESSIONALIZATION

Peer help was key to the early philosophy of empowerment, but that priority eroded over time. A number of earlier volunteers and staff noted the decline in women helping women as the challenges for clients became more difficult to negotiate and the women more culturally diverse. At the same time, the staff became more professional as volunteering declined (women's need for paid work increased) and the need for specialized knowledge and skills on staff increased, especially in areas of substance abuse and mental health. The most notable example of peer help in T House's services today is in the community, where groups of women are meeting with T House staff and talking about their experiences. The emergency shelter, whose residents are the most dislocated and lack "normal" supports, may be the least likely context for peer help.

FUNDING AND ITS CONSEQUENCES

Once Transition House was no longer supported exclusively by individual and local business donations, tension about funding became another persistent theme. The exception, surprisingly, is the original acceptance of state money from DSS (now DCF) through The Coalition (now Jane Doe). Perhaps this was because Coalition members believed their solidarity and the recognition of their expertise allowed them to "call the shots," and they were not very seriously monitored in the early days.

Now the organization is largely dependent on government grants, each of which has specific requirements for its use and specific requirements for reporting. To negotiate with funders is challenging, and it is difficult to know how or how much to "push back." Dependence on grants has two apparent consequences that are costly. First, Transition House must invest considerable time and effort to continually apply for necessary resources; second, the organization must maintain accountability to funders whose demands may be out of touch with the realities of clients' situations, agency priorities, or both. It will take very creative thinking, and maybe organizing, to escape the cycle—sometimes the tyranny—of grant applications and funders' demands. In a culture that is not willing to support services for its neediest members, the funding problem is shared by a great many small organizations that individually and collectively play an essential role.

BOUNDARIES

In the early years, boundaries between and among those involved directly with the organization were, by conviction, extremely porous. Boundaries between T House and other community organizations, on the other hand, were relatively closed, except to other movement organizations. In that context, starting in the 1980s, the DVIP became the "ambassador" for Transition House to the rest of Cambridge and the state. Gradually, as the structure of the agency changed, the boundaries around different groups internal to Transition House have become less porous and the boundaries with the rest of the city and state much more so. With less insularity, collaboration is much more possible, and new collaborations are a hallmark of the current era.

Close relationships among board, staff and long-time volunteers had, in many ways, sustained T House, and also those who staffed and ran it. The current clear administrative structure (ED, management team), outsider board, relative absence of volunteer staff in administrative or most client service roles, and increasingly collaborative relationships in the community represent a big change.

CULTURE, RACE, AND CLASS

People involved with Transition House have always paid explicit attention to issues of race and class. What Risa notes today was true from the beginning: "We are more willing than most organizations to deal with the messiness of class, race, gender." Founded by poor women, it was soon staffed primarily by less poor women whose privilege was a focus in the collective's attention to class. Founded by white women, and staffed primarily by white women, Transition House sought and hired people of color in an effort to transcend its white cultural bias. Nonetheless, in the early 2000s a board member of color saw it as having "white culture, mainstream cultural norms." The most difficult staff grievances in the 1990s and 2000s involved accusations of racism. Today the staff and the residents are broadly multicultural, and the staff continues to work against implicit dominant cultural bias.

GENDER

In the beginning, the organization was very much concerned with gender. T House was a women's space; it was fundamentally by, for, and about women, part of the larger women's movement of the 1970s to establish the power of women to govern their own lives without the need for male support. No one at Transition House talks that way today, although they recognize and respect its feminist history.

Most of Transition House's clients are women and children dealing with nearly insurmountable obstacles to the kinds of lives they wish to live. Some of these obstacles can be seen as "women's issues," such as the lack of affordable/free day care for small children, as well as the lower status and pay of "women's work," even when done by men. Many are less obviously gender-related, e.g., language and literacy barriers, immigration status, lack of affordable housing, and lack of jobs with sufficient wages to sustain a household. Even those are illuminated if viewed through a gender lens, but a radical movement for these women needs to go beyond fighting patriarchy. One staff person believes, "T House should educate itself more on radical issues that affect our clients—what kinds of meetings, rallies you go to. Patriarchy is still a huge part, but it [doesn't exist in a silo]." The radical movement needed to liberate today's Transition House residents from the oppressive conditions of their lives is not the radical women's movement of the 1970s.

A Personal Conclusion

I took on this project with no idea that it would get as big as it did. Thanks to the generosity of all those who gave papers and gave time, there was a lot of information. As importantly for me, I had the privilege of conversation with many terrific women (and a couple of men). I heard their devotion to Transition House, their frustrations with Transition House, and (almost always) the importance of Transition House in their lives. It is difficult to convey the depth of feeling held by so many people who played a role in the history of this organization, or how big a role the organization played in so many people's personal histories.

Transition House's original purpose of providing refuge for women fleeing domestic violence was part of its larger purpose of changing the culture through empowering women. Over the years, those dual purposes, of providing shelter and support *and* changing the culture, were not easily integrated and often were in tension with each other. Nonetheless, through four decades Transition House never abandoned those who came to it for refuge and continually developed innovative programs.

The Transition House of today is a more complex and evolved version of its 1975 self; and its organizing principles, organization, and relation to the environment look quite different. To return to the inelegant question of the introduction: What happened? Here are what I see as parts of the answer:

- The very successes of the late 1970s into the 1990s (increased public awareness of domestic violence, organizational training on issues for survivors, new legislation and funding resources) changed Transition House's relationships with mainstream institutions and culture. To maintain an embattled stance became unnecessary and, at the cost of needed resources and relationships, even unwise.

- We know more about intimate violence than we did in the 1970s, and it turns out to be more complicated than it seemed. Escape is not always the solution; the ties that bind may be strong and persistent, even when the relationship is dangerous. People's lives are many-faceted, and domestic violence is rarely "the" problem; true respect is not conveyed by addressing one facet alone. Women are also capable of intimate violence. The criminal justice system is not the best (or even a useful) recourse for many women.

- Our country's policies are more regressive than they were in the 1970s. That's the only simple way to put it. It has become more difficult to get out of poverty. T House was not founded about poverty. Although the founders were women on welfare, it did not look like poverty was an overriding issue in 1975. In the beginning, at least as reported then and remembered now, shelter residents were from all social classes, with the common experience of escaping violence. That is not true today. Intimate violence occurs in all social classes, but the women (and occasionally men) who come to T House are almost always poor.

- The people coming for support now often have very different experiences from the women who were coming in the 1970s. T House's mission is concerned with intimate violence, but today its practice is also related to poverty, jobs, wages, housing, education, child care, immigration, and health care including services for substance misuse and mental health. A movement for radical social change that speaks to today's women's experience needs to address more than patriarchy.

I disagree with those I interviewed who believe the work, in the end, accomplished nothing, given how prevalent domestic violence remains. When I was a "battered wife" in the 1960s, there was no such concept, no hotlines, no shelters. In the disadvantaged community in which I worked some people recognized my bruises for what they were and clearly felt that was part of what women sometimes have to endure. In the privileged community in which I lived, people believed my lies about accidents—abuse of a wife by a husband was not on their mental radar or was (literally) unspeakable. Each survivor felt alone. I know that survivors today have a better chance of being *seen* and *heard*, and getting support. I hope the same is true for abusers.

Transition House was a leader in bringing us to consciousness about women's oppression and, particularly, violence against women. It has been a leader in recognizing the needs of children who witness violence in the home and the possibilities of preventing intimate violence through education of our youth. Today it is an innovator in creative collaboration, particularly with the city. It has never abandoned its commitment to women fleeing violence, even as that commitment required new forms of organization and new kinds of programs and efforts. Transition House has always attracted amazing people to its work. Remarkable people are there now, carrying on. I feel fortunate and privileged to be their ally in this work.

Acknowledgements

The following people (listed alphabetically by first name) gave generously of their time for interviews and/or follow-up information:

Amy Yamashita
Bill Stanton
Carole Sousa
Celeste Lepinasse
Cherie Jimenez
Chris Butler
Chris Womendez
Cindy Bridger
David Adams
Elsbeth Kalendarian
Ester Serra Luque
Fatimah
Faraz Sabet
Francis Bridger
Fred Berman
Gail Sullivan
Genet Bekele
Gwyn Helie
Janet Donovan
Jasmine Khalfani
Jean Rioux
Jenny Herrera
Joanne McEachern
Joyce King

Judie Blair
Judith Moore
Judy Clark
Judy Norris
Julie Kahn-Schaye
Kara Blue
Karla
Katherine Triantifillou
Larissa MacFarquhar
Libby Bouvier
Liz McAuliffe
Liz Speakman
Linda Chadwick
Linda McMaster
Lisa Leghorn
Lor (Laurie) Holmes
Lorna Peterson
Lucinda
Lurena Lee
Lynne
Maria Chavez
Marjorie Decker
Mary Gilfus
Mary Tiseo

Mercedes Thompkins
Meredith Weenick
Mimi Graney
Molly Lovelock
Nan Hong
Nancy Ryan
Nanette Veilleux (Simenas)
Norma Wassel
Patti Cullen
Rachel Burger
Renae Scott Gray
Risa Mednick
Robin Braverman

Ronit Barkai
Seung Hee Jeong
Shameka Gregory
Shayla Simmons
Stephanie Poggie
Susan Pacheco
Susan Yanow
Tonie Mondesir
Valerie Druckenmiller
Venus Taylor
Wylie Doughty
Yves-Rose SaintDic
Zohar Fuller